The Presidential Briefings Series
Robert J. Spitzer, Series Editor

The Presidential Briefings Series provides concise and readable introductions to topics of concern to those who have been and will be President of the United States. By approaching their subjects from the vantage point of what a president most needs to know, and what the citizenry most need to know about the presidency, these books are authoritative and significant works on subjects related to the presidency.

Previously published and forthcoming works include:

Political Rhetoric by Mary E. Stuckey
Making Foreign Policy Decisions by Christopher J. Fettweis
Presidential Leadership in an Age of Change by Michael A. Genovese
Picking Judges by Nancy Maveety

PRESIDENTIAL BRIEFINGS

Picking Judges

NANCY MAVEETY

Routledge
Taylor & Francis Group
LONDON AND NEW YORK

First published 2016 by Transaction Publishers

Published 2017 by Routledge
2 Park Square, Milton Park, Abingdon, Oxon OX14 4RN
711 Third Avenue, New York, NY 10017, USA

Routledge is an imprint of the Taylor & Francis Group, an informa business

Library of Congress Catalog Number: 2015043184

Library of Congress Cataloging-in-Publication Data

Names: Maveety, Nancy, author.
Title: Picking judges / Nancy Maveety.
Description: New Brunswick : Transaction Publishers, 2016.
Identifiers: LCCN 2015043184| ISBN 9781412862745 (hardcover) | ISBN 9781412863308 (pbk.)
Subjects: LCSH: Judges--Selection and appointment--United States.
Classification: LCC KF8776 .M337 2016 | DDC 347.73/2034--dc23
LC record available at http://lccn.loc.gov/2015043184

ISBN-13: 978-1-4128-6274-5 (hbk)
ISBN-13: 978-1-4128-6330-8 (pbk)

In memory of my colleague and my old friend,
Tom Langston

CONTENTS

Introduction		ix
1	History	1
2	Candidates	35
3	Context	53
4	How	85
5	Why	105
Bibliography		119

INTRODUCTION

This short volume, styled as a presidential briefing book, attempts to convince the reluctant or the misinformed that a president can and must "pack the courts." In exercising the executive's Article II power to nominate federal judicial candidates for confirmation by the Senate, a president has the opportunity to leave a policy legacy that far outlasts the tenure of his or her administration. But legacies do not come cheap, and to make successful appointments, a president must husband as well as spend political resources, assess and set both short- and long-term goals, and attend to the legislative environment and federal bench situation with which he or she is faced.

While some presidential advisors might counsel against wasting political capital on a minimally significant part of the presidential agenda, this briefing book explains how and why such advice should be taken with a grain of salt. Beginning with a chapter that reviews the historical evolution and development of the president's Article II appointment power with respect to the federal courts, the discussion then turns to a description of the key transformational events and moments that serve as historical and systemic mileposts—or teaching moments, for future chief executives and their staff. A second chapter builds on these lessons of history to examine the various qualities and qualifications that a president considers in his or her candidates for nomination to the federal bench. The correct mix of political, legal, professional, personal, and demographic characteristics not only reduces informational uncertainty about the future on-the-bench performance of prospective appointees, but also points to the relative political *and electoral* costs *and payoffs* that are the consequences of choosing particular kinds of nominees.

The third chapter is directed at the timorous and addresses assessing the politico-institutional context in which a president must work to secure the *successful confirmation* of his or her judicial candidates. Understanding this context and the factors within it allows a president to reduce the political uncertainty as to his or her nominees' confirmation prospects—allowing the president to calculate when and when not to act boldly in filling vacancies on the federal bench, from the US Supreme Court to the courts of appeal to the federal district courts. A fourth chapter constructs a "how to" of ingredients and steps that a president can adapt to his or her particular circumstances and act upon in light of the lessons of Chapters 1–3. Specifically, the chapter recommends and details the twin processes of *candidate screening* and *executive staffing*—with carefully selected members of the latter engaging in the identifying of the former. Finally, a fifth chapter takes this briefing book to the "why" question and takes on the contrarian who still might need convincing as to the importance of the president's judicial appointment efforts. It is here that the issue of presidential legacy is directly confronted, with a candid account of both the policy-oriented model of judging that is the contribution of contemporary political science and a frank acknowledgment that elections have consequences coming together to endorse presidential agency *vis a vis* the federal courts. A president's active use of the scope of the powers of the office, including judicial appointment, ensures that law is—and continues to be—shaped by changing coalitions of policy interests.

Agency is legacy.

ONE

History

If history is any guide, it should be for the president, in selecting nominees to staff the federal judiciary. What a history of the constitutional origins and presidential utilization of the Article II appointment power teaches is that the formal, constitutional process is the baseline constraint from which presidents can operate to create opportunities, or foreclose them.

This chapter describes the historical evolution and development of the president's Article II appointment power with respect to the federal judiciary, outlining the institutional dynamics of presidential nomination and senatorial advice and consent in confirmation. The constitutional framework is presented as the formal baseline from which and within which presidential discretion and leadership can operate. Mileposts, both historical and systemic, in the development of the formal dimensions of the judicial appointment power are briefly illuminated. That development, as we shall see, is a matter of not only the expansive utilization, but also the disadvantageous misuse, of options—those presented and those made.

The following transformational moments and events structure the discussion of mileposts in the exercise of judicial appointment power: (1) cardinal criteria of the early period, from the presidency of George Washington through that of Andrew Jackson: party loyalty and geography of appointees; (2) the Senate gets political: Andrew Johnson and the shrinking of the court; (3) the contentious confirmation of Louis Brandeis: organized political opposition meets presidential conceptions of merit in appointees; (4) Franklin Delano Roosevelt, the court-packing plan, and executive dominance of the court; (5) Richard Nixon's appeal to the electorate: his campaign for "strict constructionists"; (6) ideology, interest group activism, and courting the media: the watershed that is the Robert Bork nomination; and (7) institutional conflict and the modern "nuclear option": partisan polarization and its impact on the judicial appointment process.

The Constitutional Framework of Article II

The relationship between the presidency and the federal judiciary is not among the most copiously delineated in the constitutional system of separation of powers and checks and balances. While it was assumed that there be a federal judiciary and that it be one of separate and independent powers, and while there was some debate at the Constitutional Convention in Philadelphia as to who should appoint the federal judges, the chief concern of the state delegates was not to replicate the overweening authority the British crown had had over its appointed judicial officers in the American colonies. Executive dominance of judicial appointment was thus distrusted, but so was exclusive legislative control of judicial selection. The scheme of presidential nomination with the advice and consent of the Senate was adopted in the closing days of discussion and represented a compromise between the nationally centralizing impetus of the Federalist delegates and the regional influence and state-level participation championed by their opponents.

What the appointive system was most directly engineered to guarantee was judicial independence. The exact qualities or criteria in candidates for appointment were left unspecified; judges' independence was thus institutionally derived rather than personally assured. To this end, the shared appointive powers of the executive and the legislature were phrased as such in section 2 of Article II, describing the powers of the president:

> ". . . he [the president] shall nominate, and by and with the advice and consent of the Senate, shall appoint . . . judges of the Supreme Court, and all other officers of the United States,

> whose appointments are not herein otherwise provided for, and which shall be established by law"

> The particular formulation in section 2, explicitly mentioning only the judges of the Supreme Court as part of this shared appointment process, is the result of the vague accounting of the national judicial branch in Article III, whose section 1 sets out only:

> "The judicial power of the United States shall be vested in one Supreme Court, and in such inferior courts as the Congress may from time to time ordain and establish."

The section continues that "the judges shall hold their offices during good behavior." This protection of tenure in office, presumably for life, combined with the joint appointive actions by the president and the Senate, ensured that judges were not beholden to either for their continuation in office and could perform their duties without fear of arbitrary or retaliatory removal—with political independence, in other words.

Still, a reality of the combined import of the two constitutional clauses is that Congress as a whole retains a great deal of authority over the structure and the content of the federal judicial branch. Inferior courts are left to the legislature to define, as are the number of Supreme Court judges; the first Congress did both in the Judiciary Act of 1789 and continued to articulate such parameters in subsequent acts. The president, therefore, affects the composition but not the construction of the federal courts. Moreover, the unelaborated senatorial "advice and consent" would prove to be much greater than a perfunctory approval role, with the full Senate taking a very active interest in the judges nominated for service on the federal courts, inferior and Supreme. This was partly because, for many decades, Supreme Court judges' duties included "riding circuit": sitting, with federal district (inferior) judges located in states, to form appellate courts of review for those federal trial court decisions issued in that geographic area. Each Supreme Court judge, or justice, had a territorial jurisdiction that fell within the shared purview of the senators of various neighboring states. So a Supreme Court appointment was a vital state interest, and members of the Senate did not hesitate to *advise* presidents. Judicial selection was thus linked, initially, to a regional distribution pattern and the size of the court to the number of federal circuits. And, notwithstanding the senatorial interest in who would serve as judge on the state's regional federal circuit court, senatorial *consent* very quickly took the form of a confirmation vote, up or down, on the president's proffered judicial candidates—affecting one of the early nominations to the Supreme Court, by President Washington, of John Rutledge, who was ultimately rejected as a replacement chief justice even though he ended up serving several months as a recess appointment.

The takeaway point, in reviewing the constitutional framework and its origins, is that the formal outline of the federal judicial selection process circumscribed presidential authority—both in its original purpose and its initial operations.

Mileposts: Transformational Moments and Events

The first period of presidential judicial selection, from the presidency of George Washington through that of Andrew Jackson, set a template for both nomination and confirmation criteria and the politics of inter-branch relations with respect to staffing the federal judiciary. From early on, two criteria stood out in presidential identification of nominees and senatorial evaluation of them: party loyalty or identity, and geographic or regional representation. Washington, in particular, faced the special challenge of establishing a precedent, both for the respectability of the new judicial branch and for the presidential role in shaping its membership. The pursuit of excellence in candidates was his overarching motif; likewise, their support and advocacy of the Constitution, as Federalists like himself, was critical to their qualification as potential judges. A candidate's geographic home also strongly influenced Washington, for two reasons. First, as Henry Abraham remarks in his seminal study *Justices and Presidents*, the first president regarded geographic appointments "as extremely important in light of his constant endeavor to be president of *all* the states of the fledgling nation, and he repeatedly expressed his desire to see each section 'represented' on the Supreme Court" (3rd ed., pp. 78–9 [emphasis in original]). The strategic use of judicial appointment to bind the states together into the federal system was behind this concern for representativeness, just as rewarding strategic states—electorally for the party or, more contemporaneously, for the ratification of the Constitution—could be accomplished with a seat on the highest court. But there was a second, equally functionalist purpose to considerations of geography: the Supreme Court justices, for most of the first century of their service on the institution, had the critical state-based duties of sitting in circuit with state-located district judges as part of appellate court review panels. As those circuits and a justice's share of the work were defined by region, the justice's home state mattered, for he was not only an emissary of the national government but also a local son familiar with and sympathetic to that circuit's particular kinds of legal cases and controversies.

What Washington understood, but some of his successors over the decades did not, was that loyalty to the party cause is best tempered with stature as a jurisprudential figure. While no one can fault the second president John Adams for selecting the great and truly first *Chief* Justice John Marshall, Adams nevertheless struggled to convince a Senate *controlled by his own party* to accept a candidate without judicial experience or apparent aptitude. (Marshall seemingly possessed neither.) James Madison, in particular, had something of a checkered run with his Supreme Court appointments: parrying with Congress was not among his gifts. And both he and subsequent president John Quincy Adams suffered the indignity (or simply the setback) of having successfully confirmed nominees then decline the position on the high court. (Adams, indeed, declined such from Madison himself.) The pled lack of legal competence and/or bigger fish to fry politically seemed to be the reasons, and even Washington had at times struggled to pitch a Supreme Court seat as sufficiently attractive to ambitious, policy-minded politicians.

Only with the tenure of Andrew Jackson did the first period of presidential judicial selection fully flower from its

Washingtonian seed. Jackson's term of office saw an adroit presidential wielding of the candidate qualities of party loyalty, geographic identity, and affinity for the judicial institution to select judges who both served political purposes and promoted judicial branch sovereignty. Without the latter institutional affinity, a president's judicial appointees cannot fully realize the presidential aspiration to use the courts to further partisan and administration objectives. Washington had of course seen this opportunity and attempted to exploit it, but the uncertain juridical capability and ensuing unappealing career path of the federal judiciary partially stymied the efforts of early presidents.

Jackson's presidency (1829–36) would fulfill the appointive precedent set during Washington's (1789–1800). His nominations sharpened the notion of presidential partisan goals, even while he hewed carefully to geographic considerations. Indeed, regional sectionalism overlaid with party strife combined with assertive congressional leaders to complicate and occasionally confound Jackson's appointee choices. But his partisan fellows were almost all uniformly capable political actors who proved to be shrewd and skillful judicial actors, including his choice for the next chief justice, Roger Brooke Taney. And as congressional legislation enlarged the size of the Supreme Court in creating new circuits to serve the expanding nation of newly admitted states, Jackson and his handpicked successor Martin Van Buren carefully balanced shared party vision with regional appropriateness.

Regional conflict, the division between agrarian slave and commercial free states, and the coming Civil War between the secessionist South and the unionist North, would of course make presidential considerations for geographical balance in staffing the federal judiciary seem rather quaint. The period following Jacksonianism and into the Civil War and the presidency of Abraham Lincoln is, presidential judicial appointment-wise, a period of heightened congressional insurgency and sectional sectarianism. Presidential challenges of finding nominees who would unify disparate groups took various forms but characterized the judicial selection climate, up until the next milepost or transformational moment in the exercise of the judicial appointment power. Unlike the first "moment," which was a period and a formative one, this second milepost was an event and a transformative one.

For the purpose of this chapter's history of the development of the president's Article II appointment power, we call this event "the Senate gets political." The president on the receiving end of these senatorial maneuvers in advice and consent was the unfortunate and minimally talented figure of Andrew Johnson. The story that this milepost event reveals is that a less-than-capable president can substantially worsen disadvantageous circumstances. The Johnson episode, which congeals around his single and unsuccessful Supreme Court nomination, highlights the ever-shifting territory of inter-branch relations with respect to federal judicial appointment. A president neglects institutional dynamics and senatorial power at his peril.

The Judiciary Act of 1866 is the centerpiece of a Johnson story of congressional retaliation for presidential obstruction of powerful Republican party operatives and their objectives to define and execute Reconstruction as a policy—a story that of course includes articles of impeachment voted and proceeding one vote shy of conviction. But the Johnson story is also a lesson as to the constitutionally supplied pitfalls of any period of congressional assertiveness. The Act of 1866 responded to Johnson's effort to name a replacement for a vacant Supreme Court seat by reducing the size of the body from ten to nine and then, by the next natural attrition, to eight. What the act communicates, first and foremost, is that *Congress controls* the number of justices, the number of potential presidential appointees. Article III is silent on this, just as it leaves to congressional disposition—in every sense of the word—the structuring of the personnel who will make up the federal judiciary. A vigorous Congress will take advantage of such opportunities—just as a series of dominant Senates used the confirmation power to frustrate the judicial nominations of a series of compromised presidents in the decades leading up to Lincoln's momentous election in 1860. Congress ascendant poses a significant constitutional threat to an unwary or inept president, as proposals in 1867 and 1868 to place judicial selection entirely in legislative hands unsubtly suggest.

The Judiciary Act of 1866, as an anti-Johnson measure, also signifies the reality of the Senate's own partisan appointment goals with respect to the federal judiciary. While its advice and consent were never pro forma, the act to reduce court size and essentially take away from a sitting president future staffing options demonstrates that a mobilized congressional party—as the Radical Republicans were in this era—can and will seek to secure an advantage and an advantageous voice for its own preferred appointees. (Freezing court size during this time period kept in place a sizeable majority of safely pro-Lincoln justices.) Senators, in other words, can have political or ideological appointment objectives just as much as presidents can. Senators are, moreover, equipped with weapons in the constitutional system—weapons of their own body and as part of Congress—to effectuate those objectives. The constitutional framework is a formal baseline from which *senatorial* as well as presidential discretion and leadership can operate: the painful teaching moment that the Senate getting political was for President Johnson. Presidential appointment opportunity foreclosed says it all, without quite saying enough to describe the defeat that was his.

If the aforementioned milepost event was a systemic milepost that advanced the formal baseline sketched by the Constitution to the Senate's advantage, the next milepost in the evolution of judicial appointive power was an event that integrated historical changes of a political cultural variety. These changes were the rise of organized group interests in American politics, new ethnic and religious demographics for a new, twentieth-century nation, and new notions of professional merit in the Progressive era that challenged the old political order. All three of these society-wide phenomena combined to touch and to shape the contentious confirmation of Supreme Court nominee Louis Brandeis. Appointed in 1916 by President Woodrow Wilson after a bitter political battle filled with borderline defamatory accusations, Brandeis was the first Jewish justice to serve on the high court. As a candidate, he was subjected to charges of political radicalism, scurrilous assaults on his character, and anti-Semitism. Historically speaking, his appointment would highlight a new chapter in the judicial selection process: the role of organized political opposition in the operation of advice and consent.

His nomination also earmarked a new presidential aspiration for judicial candidates: political fealty demonstrated in innovative and impactful legal advocacy. Progressives like Wilson never discarded the notion of party-political compatibility between themselves and their nominees, but the Progressives as a political movement were less tied to the strictures of partisanship and more open to considering a potential appointee's "real" politics and a broad range of "political" activities as qualifications. Brandeis' success and distinction as an advocate for social justice and his path-breaking use of sociological data in his appellate briefs brought Brandeis acclaim as the People's Lawyer, caught the attention of the president who esteemed his counsel on policy matters, and drew the ire of the pro-business interests who labeled him a dangerous radical. Brandeis was a new kind of judicial candidate, in several different ways. He represented the force of political progressivism in law and a stance toward law and courts as engines of social change and reform. He was, in that sense, an activist legal intellectual. He also reflected the more diverse ethnic and religious demographics of the United States at the turn of the twentieth century, as immigration patterns shifted and new urban population centers and new urban elites developed. Both aspects of his background inspired an organized opposition to his nomination of a kind that had never been seen before.

Antipathy to his reformist politics and anti-Semitic feelings combined into a campaign led by conservative forces in American industry and finance and their allies in the professional bar; sympathetic senators hostile to Wilson's agenda united with prominent, pro-business newspapers such as the *Wall Street Journal* and the *Los Angeles Times* to denounce Brandeis' professionalism and temperament. The suspicion, of course, was that he was a dangerous radical: a socialist critic of the capitalist system and a practitioner of a sociological jurisprudence that advantaged the cause of pro-labor, egalitarian reform. His patriotism was impugned, which was deeply unfair, and a measure of the threat his legal progressivism posed to conservative Republican orthodoxy. While not derailed, his appointment was delayed for more than four months by endless hearings and witness testimony. Indeed, Brandeis' selection marked the first time that the Senate Judiciary Committee held public investigative hearings on a nominee—not coincidentally, a public exercise following quickly on the heels of the ratification of the Seventeenth Amendment and the subjection of senators to direct popular election.

Senatorial opponents used the new confirmation procedure to call witnesses they hoped would malign the candidate's character and scuttle his appointment. Yet many senators were themselves reluctant to speak out against the nominee, due to Brandeis' widespread popular support and almost folk-hero status. In the end, that, and his steadfast presidential support prevailed, with 47–22 senators voting to confirm and twenty-seven not voting at all.

As *Confirmation Wars* author Benjamin Wittes writes, "While interest groups had played a role in prior nominations, the Brandeis nomination marked a significant procedural step toward the modern system: Popularly elected senators had begun investigating nominees with one eye on their constituents" (2006, 48). Did pro-business interests and elites hold captive the senators who mounted this investigative campaign? Interest group scholars would argue that this period of American political history, at the turn of the twentieth century, saw rising levels of political corruption as industry trusts and monopolies sought to use the political and legal systems to enshrine statutory advantages for (or, more often, prevent statutory disadvantages to) their economic hegemony. Judicial interpretations of the Constitution that protected economic rights such as the liberty of contract were sought as part of these advantages, turning business elites and their senatorial avatars into an organized interest in opposition to judicial candidates who supported governmental authority to pursue regulatory reform. Senators' "constituents" were thus the dominant, organized special interests that defined senatorial electoral politics by controlling state party politics and, thus, sought to influence judicial confirmation politics. Yet labor and populist forces could also sway an electorate; ultimately, it was fear of and reaction to this opinion favoring Brandeis that turned so many senators craven or weakly supportive.

Ironically, though Brandeis was finally appointed and served with great distinction, the conflict between organized opposition and intellectual merit that threatened to warp and even jeopardize his confirmation would discomfit many a future president to compromise on the latter. Selecting visionary thinkers or leading-light litigators and facing the prospect of an organized political opposition, networked between legislators, their special interests sponsors, and their press outlets, was something few presidents undertook, lightly or at all. But as a result of the Seventeenth Amendment, presidential calculations in the matter were now remarkably similar to those of senators: both branch actors needed the organized political support that would translate into popular electoral support for their actions regarding judicial nominees. Presidents had always needed for their nominees to be talismans of presidential leadership, of the party-in-government and the party-in-the-electorate. Now, senators too were mindful of the reaction of organized interests in and with an effect on their state electorates, to their positions on presidential judicial candidates. The Brandeis case, as a first of its kind, displayed a president who had calculated correctly, but riskily. Senatorial opponents, initially empowered by the organized anti-Progressive interests, were in the end too leery of public backlash to go on record against him—instead "encourag[ing] others (notably lawyers and bar associations) to denounce Brandeis" (Maltese 1995, 51). Still, the lesson of the Brandeis appointment was less one of victory and defeat than of the new style of rendering advice and consent: organized interests could and would mount a political opposition to presidential judicial nominees, and senators would and could formally integrate such organized opposition into the more publically open confirmation process. Interest groups, including bar associations, became an inescapable part of the inter-branch dynamic.

The pro-business Republican coalition that attempted to defeat Wilson's judicial champion needed to wait only an election cycle before taking the White House in a "return to normalcy" that saw the appointment of a series of justices with backgrounds as corporate lawyers and economically conservative philosophies. It was this lineup of judicial personnel and the legal policy of their decisions that set the stage for the next milepost in appointment power politics: a moment in inter-branch conflict that disrupted and altered the balance of power between executive and Senate.

Meantime, several institutional changes had occurred for the Supreme Court. First, its numbers had stabilized in the later decades of the nineteenth century, with nine justices being the accepted convention. And no longer did its members have to match the number of circuits and engage in circuit court duties: with the passage of the Judiciary Act of 1891, Congress created the circuit courts of appeal and established nine intermediate appellate courts staffed with new federally appointed judges. This second major institutional change sought to relieve the Supreme Court's ballooning caseload, the result of the proliferation of litigation resulting from the rapid industrialization of the nation and the beginnings of regulatory legislation. The new circuit courts of appeal undertook a major portion of mandatory appeals from the district courts below and were the final arbiters of the many diversity jurisdiction cases in which parties were from different states. Finally, the Judiciary Act of 1925 or the "Judges' Bill" further scaled back the Supreme Court's docket to make it a largely discretionary appellate review court. The measure was promoted as an administrative efficiency reform and response to the court's still heavy workload in error correction in ordinary private litigation. The Judges' Bill converted the Supreme Court into a constitutional and statutory tribunal that resolved public policy issues of national importance. These structural and institutional changes had a noteworthy impact on presidential judicial appointment. Clearly, the creation of a new level of federal courts was a windfall of presidential selection opportunities—although at this point in the history of appointment politics, lower federal court judgeships were relatively small potatoes for most presidents and home state senators jealously guarded these appointments as aspects of local party patronage. Presidents deferred to home state senators in deciding whom to nominate, because the norm of collegiality in the Senate meant that senators supported their fellow senators' preferences, a custom known as senatorial courtesy. Nevertheless, presidents had a new judicial terrain to work on with senatorial partisans, in rewarding political supporters with seats on the federal bench. Additionally, and more significantly for the long term, the conversion of the Supreme Court into a more exclusively constitutional and a national policy-directed court meant that prospective justices were of even greater consequence than before, in terms of their potential impact on a president's party's legal policy agenda.

This became pointedly clear at the next milepost in the development of the judicial appointment power. Wilson's struggle to see Brandeis confirmed had marked the emergence of organized political opposition in the operation of senatorial advice and consent. Franklin Roosevelt's struggle was with the Supreme Court itself, and the defining moment that his presidency presents was his court-packing plan. But this milepost moment, and the executive dominance of the court that it ultimately enabled, was prefigured by the defining historical moment of the Great Depression and FDR's response to it, his New Deal.

Unregulated economic development and unbridled financial speculation in the 1920s had yielded the Stock market crash of 1929. Investors' panic led to a run on banks and then the failure of the majority of financial institutions; drought and debt and bankruptcy forced a collapse of the farming sector and a deflationary spiral of wages and prices. Manufacture and its supporting industries were imperiled. The White House incumbent, Republican Herbert Hoover, had no effective response to this market crisis and its escalating social chaos. Democrat Franklin Delano Roosevelt, elected in a landslide in 1932, sought to use massively reconceived, centralized, and strengthened authority of the national government to install programs to save the private enterprise economy. His efforts, of course, included governmental intervention into "free" markets, governmental power to regulate private property in the common good, and governmental regulation of commerce that vastly expanded congressional and federal powers. He justified such measures as necessities in response to a national economic emergency, bolstered by his party's electoral mandate. The reality too, as he saw it, was that the forces of instability and imbalance in the modern national industrial economy required the countervailing force of government to induce stability, fair competition, and productivity.

The problem was the Supreme Court—or rather, a majority of justices on the Court in 1933, who strenuously opposed Roosevelt's New Deal legislative programs as violating the Constitution. Again and again, a coalition of conservative justices struck down economic recovery and relief programs as contravening constitutional limits on governmental power or interfering with persons' and corporations' property and contractual liberties. Nicknamed the Horsemen of the Apocalypse and almost all appointed by Republican presidents, these jurists blocked the president's attempted solutions and exacerbated the political conflict between two political philosophies and between the executive and judicial branches.

With no deaths or retirements, the Nine Old Men of the Supreme Court persisted into FDR's second term, continuing to obstruct most of his New Deal policies. Roosevelt was frustrated. In his annual message to Congress, delivered in January 1937, the president sounded a new note. "Difficulties have grown," he intoned, "out of [the Constitution's] interpretation; but rightly considered, it can be used as an instrument of progress, and not as a device for prevention of action." More ominously, he concluded: "Means must be found to adapt our legal forms and our judicial interpretation to the actual present national needs." In February, Roosevelt submitted to his Democrat-controlled Congress a sweeping piece of legislation designed to "reorganize" the federal judiciary to improve its efficiency. But the real target was the Supreme Court and its intransigent majority faction. The bill would grant the president authority to appoint an additional jurist for each federal judge who had served ten years or more and failed to retire after reaching his seventieth birthday. The new judges would serve alongside the existing, older judges, and with the maximum size of the High Court set at fifteen, the bill would give Roosevelt the opportunity to appoint six additional justices—thus breaking the conservative jurists' lock on the court's decisions by diluting their influence, presumably with a complement of New Deal-compliant appointees.

Of course Roosevelt presented the need for the bill more neutrally: as an effort to relieve an overburdened court and ameliorate the disabilities of old age of its "insufficient personnel." Notwithstanding this fig leaf, his proposal offended the members of the court, including those justices who had supported his measures in dissent. Their objections, and reaching out to influential Democratic senators, helped cause a storm of protest and outrage from various quarters: the bar, constitutional conservatives as well as liberals, divided members of the Democratic majority in the Senate. Newspaper editors labeled the proposal "the court-packing plan" to "retire or move over," and there was press and popular outcry to FDR's purported interference with a free and independent judiciary. The more his program to redirect the court was perceived in this way, and not as a measure to retool and manage its workload, the more opposition mounted. Public and congressional support for the bill shrank.

But it was the Supreme Court's own decisions in the spring of 1937 that really sealed the demise of the court-packing plan. In a series of narrowly decided cases, the court upheld state minimum-wage laws, the federally created National Labor Relations Board that protected the right of labor to organize collectively, and the major benefits initiative that was the Social Security Act. Branded by journalists "the switch in time that saved nine," the pro-New Deal majorities were brought about by the votes of Justice Owen Roberts and Chief Justice Charles Hughes, who realigned in these cases with the liberal members of the bench. Shortly thereafter, one of the "Four Horsemen" Justice Willis Van Devanter, announced his retirement at the end of that term. Doomed now, as many Americans saw that FDR had achieved his goals without tampering with the court's numbers, the court reorganization bill was reported negatively out of the Senate Judiciary Committee in June and sent back to committee by the full Senate in July with the recommendation to bury it.

Most political commentators, then and now, say that Roosevelt lost the legislative battle but won the war. Certainly—and somewhat stubbornly—he refused to give up on the progress of his bill even once the impetus for it had arguably passed. Less certain is the explanation for the critical shift in Justice Roberts' allegiance from the conservative jurisprudence of the judicial old guard. Was it the threat of an enlarged and potentially supine court that convinced the justices not to stand in FDR's way, or did some other factor convince some of them to adopt a more flexible understanding of the Constitution that tolerated the New Deal legislation? Or had Congress and the president begun to do a better job of crafting recovery laws that were within federal government powers?

If the court-packing plan was the battle, then executive dominance of the Supreme Court and, indeed, of federal judicial selection was the war. Through his brinksmanship—his threatening to exercise the constitutional option to increase the Court's size—Roosevelt realized presidential appointment opportunity. His was the expansive utilization of an option he himself made, and made real. This can be clearly seen in his first nominee in 1937, to replace Van Devanter: loyal New Deal supporter and senatorial Democratic champion Hugo Black. Roosevelt never wavered from the position that absolute loyalty to the principle of governmental regulatory authority and staunch adherence to an egalitarian philosophy of government and society were mandatory and appropriate qualifications for his judicial candidates—mandatory and appropriate as *policy* qualifications for his *judicial* candidates. He would go on to make eight more successful appointments, the largest number of any president save George Washington.

The milepost moment of FDR's court-packing plan and executive dominance of the court was an exercise of presidential power that disrupted and then altered the balance of power in the Article III judicial appointment process—not by any formal adjustment of branch authority but by setting a precedent of presidential action. It was, in a way, the mirror image of the Andrew Johnson episode: not a Senate ascendant, but a Chief

Executive, expansively and confidently utilizing formal appointment powers to decisively orient the federal judiciary. It is not for nothing that the phrase "packing the court" is first, foremost, and forever associated with Franklin Roosevelt, for he broke the mold of previous presidents in putting judicial selection on the presidential leadership agenda. His experience with the court in the contest over the New Deal proved that staffing the judiciary mattered; his willingness to frame presidential discretion in judicial staffing the way he did in the court-packing bill illustrated a willingness to effectuate presidential influence over judicial staff.

FDR's court-packing bill and his initiative in the judicial appointment process should be seen as creating opportunities for the exercise of presidential power. But from FDR onward, there is a fine line between such activities and enabling what comes to be known as the "Imperial Presidency." After World War II and with the growth of the executive branch, the preeminence of national party politics, and the establishment of the United States as a global superpower, the role of the American president in American governmental decision making was substantially enlarged. The president as the predominant actor in foreign affairs and domestic policy making of course has earlier antecedents: Lincoln and the Civil War, Teddy Roosevelt and the Bully Pulpit. Franklin Roosevelt's expansive use of executive powers, and his creation of an inner circle of personal staff advisors, presaged an era in which the president was not only a policy leader but also a political actor empowered by a large White House staff personally accountable to his administration and unencumbered by congressional partnership or oversight. Historian Arthur Schlesinger coined the term "imperial" in 1973 to connote a chief executive with broad latitude of action effectively checked only by a "plebiscitary" election.

If any mention of court-packing calls to mind FDR and his politics, then the term imperial presidency is redolent of Richard Nixon and his. While the saga of the Nixon presidency goes beyond the confines of this presidential briefing book, one aspect of it has relevance as a milepost in the developmental history of the Article II appointment power, as well as resembling the kind of presidential electoral politicking that Schlesinger foretold.

This next milepost was the event of Richard Nixon's 1968 presidential campaign, in which he appealed to the electorate as running *against* the current Supreme Court. Nixon's campaign marks the first time a presidential candidate made judicial appointment power a centerpiece of his candidacy, with an explicit promise to reshape the Supreme Court in his policy image. Nixon was, in essence, guaranteeing to replicate the executive dominance of the judiciary that Franklin Roosevelt had achieved. At the very least, his campaign rhetoric foregrounded for voters the critical importance of presidential influence over judicial staffing. As Kevin McMahon comments in the opening to his study *Nixon's Court*, "in the hands of Nixon, the Supreme Court became a powerful tool for attracting votes, a device for constructing a new electoral coalition" (2011, 3). Nixon's example would be influential, and far reaching.

His appeal was effective because the Warren Court of the 1960s was considered liberal and profoundly activist on a range of hot-button social issues: racial desegregation, speech rights for political dissidents and "smut peddlers" alike, the prohibition of prayer in public school, and, most significantly, expansive protection for rights of criminal defendants and the accused. Decisions such as those enshrining the *Miranda* warnings about the privilege against self-incrimination and coerced confession, and the exclusionary rule regarding the inadmissibility of evidence seized without a warrant, were wildly unpopular in some quarters—they were perceived not as civil liberties advances but as "coddling" criminals and "handcuffing" the police in the struggle to combat violent crime. Nixon pledged to appoint what he called "strict constructionists": jurists who would strictly interpret the Constitution rather than "impose their own social and political viewpoints on the American people," as he phrased it on the campaign trail in early November. His anti-Warren Court rhetoric was part of a general overture to "law and order," for the social unrest of the era had come to include urban riots, anti-Vietnam War agitation, and civil rights protest. Nixon, too, purported to speak for "the forgotten Americans," the members of the "great silent majority" who were "the non-shouters, the non-demonstrators," as he termed them. While populism and crime in the streets was and had been the currency of other candidates for office, Nixon's campaign charged that *the Supreme Court itself* was responsible for the domestic lawlessness and deterioration of the moral fabric of the nation.

Part of Nixon's motivation for the court-centered campaign strategy was to be well regarded in the South, the region that was bristling against forced bussing to integrate public schools and other national impositions on states' rights and local ways of life. He was also faced with a challenge from the right, in the form of independent candidate and former Alabama governor, the segregationist George Wallace. Between the two of them, and in their eagerness to challenge confrontationally the justices and their record of legal decision making, they "symbolized a dramatic change in how candidates spoke about the court in the midst of a presidential campaign" (McMahon 2011, 35). Much of Wallace's appeal was overtly racist, and he would prove too radical for most voters. Nixon's "Southern strategy" was combined with a clear plan to be a national candidate, taking tradition-minded voters away from Hubert Humphrey and the Democratic Party. In this, he found his critique of the court had to center on the proper role of the judiciary in American society—and the current court's transgression of that limited role.

Of course it is difficult to say definitively that his presidential campaign against the Supreme Court won Nixon the election. Still, as the candidate who wanted judges who "interpret the law and don't try to make it," Nixon successfully navigated his electoral competition, winning a narrow 302 electoral vote victory and bare popular vote lead of 43.4 percent. Importantly, he made a series of Supreme Court appointments that altered its composition—though not as sweepingly as some of his supporters might have liked. Also importantly, Nixon is responsible for two consecutive failed nominations to the high court—a topic to be taken up in subsequent chapters. But the milestone of his 1968 presidential campaign eclipses both in long-term significance: it is candidate Nixon who takes the presidential power to select the justices of the court and makes it a pointedly potent presidential campaign issue.

In a way, too, he ran a campaign in which the election was a plebiscite on the Supreme Court—with Nixon as the fixer, should the electorate render the court broken by tendering a vote for the "anti-court" candidate. This is perhaps not the plebiscitary election darkly envisioned for imperial presidents, but a "yes" vote for candidate Nixon entailed—in full or in part—the "no" vote on the Supreme Court, its judicial philosophy, and the social disorder and dismaying social change that both had allegedly unleashed. Nixon's populist outreach to the everyman unnerved by the era's unrest would have been much less evocative without the Warren Court as a target and a touchstone, and his use of the court as a campaign issue *in this way* presupposed an executive power *and ensuing popular mandate* to recalibrate its decision making. In this, Nixon completes and to a degree extends FDR's executive dominance of the court, by making executive stamping of the court a legitimate election issue and a popular expectation of elected presidents.

With Nixon's emphasis on the presidential promise to appoint justices of a particular judicial philosophy of constitutional interpretation, the concern with the "ideology" of nominees took on a new significance in judicial appointment politics. Political ideology as agreement with a president's party and its overall objectives had of course never been absent from judicial selection and the consideration of potential nominees. But beginning with FDR's struggle with a Supreme Court whose justices refused to behave with judicial restraint and legislative deference, and continuing through Nixon's salvos against Warren Court activism, judicial ideology took on a different meaning: that of a judge's constitutional philosophy, or approach to interpreting the meaning of constitutional rights, liberties, and limitations on governmental action. When Nixon spoke of "strict construction," he and his allies meant an attitude toward adapting and updating provisions of the Constitution. Its alternative of "loose" construction was associated with the idea of a "living Constitution" and the authorization of judge-led political change. Proponents of the living Constitution tended to be constitutional and political liberals, with strict constructionists likely the opposite: politically conservative and leaning toward limiting judicial discretion to interpret the Constitution's commands in light of contemporary needs and problems. Constitutional conservatism, in its backlash against the Warren Court era and subsequent decisions such as *Roe v. Wade* in 1973, increasingly embraced a philosophy or a theory of constitutional "originalism" or original intent. According to this understanding, to strictly construe the Constitution is to hew closely to the originally intended meaning of its words. This constitutional theory—or judicial "ideology," if you will—strongly affected the Republican Party with the ascendency of its right wing and in the wake of Nixon's disappointing performances, in securing appointment of his Supreme Court nominees and otherwise. Democrats and political liberals clung to a constitutional liberalism, an ideology of the living Constitution and the judicial role to carry that out, as their preferred ideology for prospective judges.

None of this became explicit, however, until the moment of the next milepost in judicial appointment politics. That moment coincides with the Ronald Reagan White House, and the creation of an administration team devoted to judicial selection. This concerted attention to the screening, scrutinizing, and "selling of Supreme Court nominees" was born of the commitment to judicial appointments as a key element of the presidential agenda. FDR had added judicial selection to the presidential leadership agenda; Nixon had advertised it; Reagan institutionalized it. This institutionalized commitment to selecting "the right" judges was new, and central to Reagan's Justice Department and the vision of his first attorney general, Edwin Meese. It was both intellectual and practical. And the commitment would also yield—in the moment and forever afterwards—charges of ideological litmus-testing, high-stakes confrontations in Senate confirmation hearings, and interest group-led mass media campaigns waged for/against judicial candidates. The transformational moment—the milepost at the crux of the Reagan agenda for the federal judiciary—partakes of all three. It is the nomination and failed confirmation of Judge Robert Bork.

Nixon's successful campaigning against the court is a milepost for future chief executives to emulate; Reagan's unsuccessful nomination of Bork is also, in its own strange way, a milepost to model, as chief executives consider how to choose, frame, and sponsor their preferred candidates for the federal judiciary. The Bork experience is a watershed moment in American politics: nothing about the president appointment power looks the same after Ronald Reagan and Robert Bork. Yet the Bork nomination, which turned so critically on the candidate's judicial ideology, did build on previous developments in the judicial appointment politics saga. One has already been mentioned: the Nixonian identification of judicial philosophy as an advertised presidential objective in staffing the courts. Two others are legacies of, or fallout from, the equally contentious but differently addressed Brandeis appointment in 1916; each sets up the context of the controversy over Bork and how the 1987 nomination and negative confirmation vote played out.

The earlier, Brandeis milepost event possessed two characteristics that come to greater fruition in the Bork milepost moment. First is the role and importance of interest group activism to the process and the outcome. The controversial nature of Brandeis' candidacy precipitated an organized opposition in the confirmation process; this opposition acted through the members of the Senate who were susceptible to political pressure from its interests, who were largely industry and financial elites against regulations on business. Their "organization" was as like-minded special interests that used money and political influence to dominate state party politics and control senators who depended on the support of those state party organizations. Loosely affiliated politically, these pro-business elites were nevertheless linked in the economic sector through various trusts and combinations, as well as being allied in capturing through ownership newspapers as outlets for influencing public opinion. They formed a coordinated opposition to reform. It was against this sort of corruption of the democratic process that Progressives railed, in speech and action and, in Brandeis' case, through litigation. As we know, in the case of Brandeis the nominee, the Progressive response and popular reaction to that opposition—to reform and to his appointment to the Supreme Court—prevailed.

In the Bork context, organized interests were established, multi-issue interest groups like the American Civil Liberties Union (ACLU), the National Organization of Women (NOW), and the National Association for the Advancement of Colored People (NAACP), as well as interest group activists who emerged from grassroots organization and mass mobilization efforts specific to the judicial arena and to an anti-Bork coalition. These included public interest groups such as People for the American Way and the Alliance for Justice Judicial Selection Project. Together and overall, this constellation of interest groups would organize into a coalition with the goal of defeating the Bork nomination. A contemporaneous volume (1989) says it all in its title: *The People Rising: the Campaign Against the Bork Nomination*. Mass or popular movements and momentum was organized into a group-based campaign actively oriented toward using whatever lobbying, media, and grassroots tactics were at their disposal to influence the public and their senators in Washington. The groups' media campaign, especially, was much more coordinated and sophisticated than ever before, with a Media Task Force using polling data to identify salient issues in different parts of the country and then target different anti-Bork television advertisements based on those polls (Maltese 1995, 91). The interest group activism was thus both more formally organized and more pluralistically diffuse than in the Brandeis situation. Perhaps because of this, the opposition to Bork was not only more successful as to the confirmation outcome—it even more dramatically affected the advice and consent process in the long term.

Its transformative import notwithstanding, the Bork case is a variation on yet another interest group theme from the preceding Brandeis case. The attentive reader will recall that with Brandeis' review by the Senate, interest groups *including the bar* would become an inescapable part of the judicial appointment dynamic. The role of bar associations in the 1916 confirmation battle was, of course, largely as participants and co-conspirators in the opposition to the nominee. Lawyers in their professional associations were frequently strongly allied with corporations, industries, railroads, and banks; as tools of such entities, the bar was part of the constellation of pro-business interests. But as the twentieth century progressed, the legal profession would begin to diversify as to its clients and the political and social orientation of its members—as the career of Louis Brandeis exemplifies. Moreover, in the same period the organized bar would develop into a more professionally certified and ethically disciplined body.

As a professional organization, the national association of licensed attorneys—the American Bar Association (ABA)—formally established in 1946 its Standing Committee on Federal Judiciary. Judicial scholar Elliott Slotnick notes that the formation of the committee followed earlier unsystematic efforts by the organized bar to influence federal judicial selection. By 1948, the ABA Committee had started to evaluate the professional qualifications of federal judicial nominees and submit those evaluations to the Senate. In 1953, at the request of President Dwight D. Eisenhower, the committee began to evaluate the professional qualifications of his potential nominees. The ABA's own literature argues that Eisenhower did so to assist him in resisting growing Republican pressures to repay political debts by appointing persons who might not have the professional qualities necessary to exercise the important responsibilities of the judicial branch. Whatever the original reason, this organized interest, in the form of the organized bar, in the form of this ABA Committee, was brought *by presidential initiative* into the judicial appointment process and given a semi-formal but extra-constitutional role in it.

Practicing attorneys have various motives, professional and personal, for involvement in the choosing of federal judges. Some are outright elitist. Indeed, the ABA has been accused as being too heavily representative of the most successful, conservative elements of the bar, and its ratings of nominees too closely linked with their white male status, elite law school pedigree, and pursuit of traditional legal practices. In spite of this, the ABA

Standing Committee's performance during the Bork confirmation exhibited a more ambiguous endorsement. Although he had received a unanimous "well-qualified" rating as nominee to the federal appellate bench just five years before, when the time came to evaluate Bork as a candidate for the Supreme Court, four members of the committee found him "not qualified," and one member voted simply "not opposed." Eight members rated him "well qualified"—the highest rating a candidate can receive, but "the dissent of a substantial minority defied precedent, and thus expectations" and showed the ABA to be "a potent outside force" to the opposition's campaign, and in the appointment process in general (Pertschuk and Schaetzel 1989, 246).

The role the bar played in the Bork confirmation was vastly different than that in the Brandeis appointment, with the latter merely introducing the bar as an organizational actor in judicial appointment politics. The ABA's fortunes would rise and fall and rise again, in subsequent judicial selection episodes, but the judgment of professional peers had a permanent part to play in nomination and confirmation processes. The Bork experience made it impossible for it not to.

The role and importance of interest group activism to the judicial appointment process and the outcome was one of two characteristics of the Brandeis confirmation event that came to full fruition in the Bork milepost moment. The second, and what would ultimately prove determinative of Robert Bork's fate, is the reality that public opinion matters for *all* the elected officials in the Article II appointment process. Both presidents and senators are mindful of reelection and attend to the popular response to their judicial candidates and reaction to their positions on them, respectively. Senators' stances on the selection of Bork cannot be separated from this electoral connection, and the interest group campaign against him took full advantage of senatorial electoral vulnerabilities, perceived and real.

There are several interactive implications here. One is that interest groups use their organizational resources to call attention to a candidate's shortfalls, igniting and mobilizing public opposition that swing-state senators disregard at their peril.

The wrong confirmation vote—whether in support of or in opposition to a president's candidate—can cause critical constituencies, needed for reelection, to peel off . . . or to be peeled off, by interest groups' eager publication of a senator's untoward position. From this, senators learn that it is easier to take cues from party-relevant interest group organs, and jump on bandwagons, than it is to engage in an independent assessment of candidate qualities and qualifications. From this, presidents learn that framing is all and that it is better to preempt the potential opposition's messaging by "going public," early and often, on one's nominees. Framing is all the easier when candidates possess no "paper trail" of obvious and ideologically tinged accomplishments. Still, if "stealth" candidates backfire or cannot be found, they can be made, by careful screening and coaching. From this, judicial nominees learn (or are taught) not to repeat the disastrously outspoken performance of Judge Bork before the Judiciary Committee, and to speak in platitudes of acceptable constitutional philosophizing—itself an increasingly moving target.

Like Brandeis, Bork exemplifies the conflict presidents face between organized opposition to and intellectual merit in their judicial candidates. Bland and palatable Bork was not; indeed, his uncompromising and unblemished ideological purity and forthright intellectual vigor was the reason Reagan picked him. As a result, stealthy he was not; post-Bork, presidents would attempt to locate less *outstanding* choices. Bork's paper trail of jurisprudential writings testified to his academic excellence, but it also removed any mystery as to what he stood for, and he spoke out at his confirmation hearings—explicitly and at length—about his views on law and policy. Such a nominee is difficult to spin, either in advance or after the fact. It is best to screen accurately, interview doggedly, pick carefully, package astutely, and promote vigorously. All of which takes an institutionalized presidential operation.

Judicial ideology, interest group activism, the dueling demagoguery of senators versus presidents, and everybody (including the nominee) "going public"—this heady brew was the milestone moment of Reagan's unsuccessful nomination of

Robert Bork. Bork's confirmation was rejected by a Senate vote of 58–42, still the largest margin of defeat for a Supreme Court candidate in history.

So how is *the Bork loss* a *milestone* in the development of presidential appointment power and a *model* for future presidents to emulate? As judicial appointments scholar John Maltese comments: ". . .the White House appeared to have been caught off guard by the groundswell of opposition to Bork, and it never regained the offensive. Presidents since then have learned the lesson and have worked closely with organized interests to mount campaigns on behalf of their nominees" (p. 138). Reagan's presidency, we must remember, is the watershed in the institutional presidency as applied to a judicial selection operation: his administration created the formal machinery of the President's Committee on Federal Judicial Selection, made up of representatives from the White House Office of White House Counsel and Justice Department Office of Legal Policy. With this institutionalized operation, "working closely with organized interests" became possible, probable, and potent. That Reagan and his team appreciated this fully only in hindsight is unfortunate for them, but edifying for future presidents. Negotiating the complexity of factors in the nomination decision and navigating the multi-actor terrain of the advice and consent process take a staff, for modern chief executives. Reagan is both the model here and the cautionary lesson.

Near-debacles in judicial appointment would continue to bedevil Reagan's successors; George H. W. Bush's selection of Clarence Thomas comes to mind, as do George W. Bush's fits and starts to name a replacement for retiring justice Sandra Day O'Connor. But Reagan's successors, Republican and Democrat, would by and large take advantage of and benefit from the machinery he put in place to facilitate presidential selection of federal judges. Outside legal advisory groups would continue to play an important role, though the ABA would find its exalted status as professional evaluator of judicial nominees under challenge during both Bush administrations, as conservative-friendly public interest law organizations such as the Washington Legal

Foundation and the Federalist Society were brought in to advise on potential candidates. Judicial selection would continue to be prominent in both presidential campaign rhetoric and presidential political agendas, and judicial ideology and candidates' legal philosophy would continue to be the focal point of presidents', senators', and interest groups' sparring. Ideological networks of politicians and think tanks would increasingly work together in identifying and assessing prospective judges, just as prospective judges would increasingly emerge from a few identifiable and reliable channels of a highly partisan-coded nature: affiliation with certain think tanks, clerkships with certain federal judges, Solicitor General's Office positions, Attorneys General or White House Counsel positions, lower federal court judgeships. Legal careers and judicial experience that promised unassailable expertise and predictable left-right alliance were preferred. Candidates who were known quantities were generally appealing to presidents of both parties, even as presidents took care that their nominees not be "Borked."

Some would argue that Reagan, in spite of the Bork miscalculation, faced little real opposition to his judicial nominees for most of his presidency, and so consistently nominated highly ideological candidates—thus provoking opposition and beginning a cycle of sorts. Ideological litmus testing became a familiar senatorial refrain in judicial appointment dynamics, the stridency of the claim not necessarily in proportion to the vigorousness of presidential efforts to shape the federal judiciary. Such rhetoric would eventually ignite presidential retaliation in kind, with chief executives charging Senate opponents with applying ideological and decisional litmus tests of their own to judicial nominees. Oratory matched and incited behavior, and vice versa. The more frequent reality of divided government, in which the president's party did not control the Senate, meant that judicial appointment politics was a game of chicken—or an outright face-off.

This oppositional stance between executive of one party and Senate of another worsened through the 2000s as partisan polarization increased throughout American society and in American government. Bipartisan compromise was difficult, across a range of issues including those subject to judicial interpretation and decision. Nixon's and Reagan's highlighting of the policy importance of staffing the courts meant that judicial nomination and confirmation was a high-stakes political endeavor, and senators took seriously as a partisan obligation the institutional opportunity to thwart presidential appointment objectives. The final milestone in the development of the president's Article II appointment power is a product of this contemporary climate of conflict and the worsening degree of senatorial obstructionism of presidential staffing prerogatives. As a period of politicized institutional conflict, partisan polarization, and contentious judicial appointment, it has antecedents in Bill Clinton's term in office but begins in earnest in the second Bush administration and spans the entire Barack Obama administration. It is the milestone of the modern "nuclear option," and it marks a political era of tit-for-tat backlashing between president and Senate, of extreme institutional uncooperativeness, and the threat of a zero-sum future of judicial staffing for the unwary chief executive.

The nuclear option milestone concerns the procedure of the filibuster and its use and abuse in the modern US Senate. A product of Senate rules, filibuster occurs when a senator attempts to delay or entirely prevent a vote on a bill by extending debate on the measure. Traditionally used in the context of law making, speech on the floor can continue until a 2/3 vote (usually 60 out of the 100 senators) brings debate to a close by invoking cloture. Practically speaking, the filibuster rule allows a Senate minority to block action in the chamber until a supermajority can be marshaled. Thus, the use or the threat to use the filibuster can affect legislation: while passage of a bill might only require a simple party-line majority, defeat or deflection of a filibuster requires a larger and potentially bipartisan coalition. Such coalition-building takes time and can consume resources, including making trade-offs in a prospective bill's substance in order to gain support for the cloture vote. Typically used infrequently, filibustering and threats to do so rose dramatically throughout the later decades of the twentieth century. Filibusters were also employed against a wider variety of proposals before the Senate. Eventually, this pattern expanded to rumblings of applying the filibuster tactic to senatorial confirmation votes, as a way of blocking or stalling presidential judicial selections.

That rumbling became more overt in 2003, when the Democratic minority in the Senate repeatedly used the filibuster to prevent a confirmation vote on Bush Sr. administration veteran and conservative lawyer Miguel Estrada, whom the president had proposed for the DC Circuit. Estrada ultimately withdrew as a nominee. Then, in 2005, another and by now credible threat to use the filibuster tactic emerged, when the Democratic minority argued that Senate rules provided for the regularization of this application of the filibuster—that the Senate's institutional responsibility to participate meaningfully in judicial appointment required it. That Democratic minority was frustrated by its inability to prevent Republican George W. Bush from populating the federal judiciary with what it considered extreme ideologues and was still chafing from GOP senators' smear tactics against Democrat Bill Clinton's first nominees for his Justice Department. Meanwhile, during the same time period, political rivalry between presidents and Senate majorities of opposing party intensified, ideological resolve stiffened, and inter-institutional relations of comity worsened. Presidents found that not only Supreme Court nominees but also lower federal court candidates were subject to a new standard of aggressive senatorial scrutiny. And opposition Senate majorities were not limited to a minority's high-drama device of the filibuster. Dilatory parliamentary tactics of different varieties were used to preclude action on confirmation of certain presidential choices—those perceived as outside the mainstream of legal thinking—as a way of forcing presidents to name less objectionable candidates. When institutional roles were reversed—when a formerly obstructionist senatorial majority party found itself in the White House and facing a Senate controlled by the opposite party previously on the receiving end of their obstruction—the pattern was replayed in retaliation. Nominees sat in confirmation limbo and some ultimately withdrew from the process; the dysfunctionality of senatorial advice and consent began to affect personnel needs within the federal courts. Yet presidents, armed with their institutionalized selection operations, and senators, inflamed with ideological and payback fervor of their own, refused to back down.

The threat to use the filibuster had been met in 2005 with the then-Senate Majority Leader's urging to use Senate rules maneuvers to declare filibustering of judicial nominees inconsistent with the constitutional grant of presidential power of appointment. This proposed declaration was named the "nuclear" option, because it would take the filibuster tactic out of confirmation politics strategizing. Senate Democrats, the Senate minority, strenuously objected to this rule change, arguing that the withdrawal of the filibuster would be used in kind and just as unfairly against a Republican minority once the Democratic Party became the majority again. (As to this they were rather prescient.) The tussling—and the stalling on Bush's nominees—continued until May of that same year, when a group of fourteen senators dubbed the "Gang of Fourteen" and consisting of seven Democrats and seven Republicans arrived at a saving compromise. The seven Democrats promised not to filibuster Bush's nominees except under "extraordinary circumstances," while the seven Republicans promised to oppose the nuclear option unless they thought a nominee was being filibustered inappropriately. The effort to ban the filibuster for confirmation votes was derailed, even though extraordinary circumstances were not defined in advance and presumably would have to be agreed upon for "appropriate" blocking of nominees to be allowed to go forward.

Phase one of the nuclear option saga was over, but the inter-branch wrangling over judicial selection was not. Democrat Barack Obama succeeded Republican President George Bush and Democrats returned to control of the Senate. Senate Republicans now carried on the deployment of legislative tactics to delay and impede confirmation of a Democratic president's lower federal court nominees. Although Obama successfully appointed two Supreme Court justices in his first term, Senate minority filibustering of prospective appointees was seriously handicapping presidential staffing in both the judicial and the executive branches. By Obama's second term, Senate Democrats—still the majority—had had enough. In November of 2013 the Senate voted 52–48 to eliminate the use of the filibuster on executive branch nominees and judicial nominees other than to the Supreme Court. With all Republicans and three Democrats voting against, the Senate had exercised the so-called nuclear option. This cleared the way for a backlog of Obama candidates to move through the process and expedited Obama's efforts to increase the proportion of his appointees in the federal judiciary.

Phase two of the nuclear option milestone—its actual implementation—would seem to advantage presidents in their utilization of their Article II appointment power, by disadvantaging the senatorial ability to object. The Senate's action created a weirdly nonconsensual kind of "advice and consent." Minority party senators, while not powerless to block a presidential choice, find their opportunities to disagree seriously diminished. Any filibustering is by definition inappropriate, or lacking "extraordinary circumstances." A very public and clearly institutional form of senatorial dissent to presidential lower court nominees was thus taken off the table. This leaves in place and makes even more likely the clandestine use of individual senatorial holds, and snarky and extra-institutional wars-of-words via interest group surrogates, as the mainstays of the Article II inter-branch appointment dynamic. Moreover, disempowering the Senate minority by defanging the filibuster in judicial confirmation scenarios was a product of party-line voting, and it promises to reward only the same. All future Senate majorities can be expected to instate the nuclear option against the Senate minority. Indeed, presidents should expect same-party-controlled Senates to exert the fullest range of their power over Senate rules, to facilitate confirmation of (party) nominees. Presidents should also expect opposite-party-controlled Senates to withhold as much consent to those nominees as their institutional branch powers permit.

The constitutional framework is a formal baseline from which senatorial as well as presidential discretion and leadership can operate: this was a lesson of the Andrew Johnson milestone, and it is a lesson of the nuclear option milestone as well. Both milestones, too, are cases of congressional initiative shaping the ever-shifting territory of inter-branch relations with respect to federal judicial appointment. Systemic mileposts in the development of the formal dimensions of the judicial appointment power, as both are, present options to presidents that can be expansively used or disadvantageously misused. Which is the nuclear option? Is this institutional modification to the formal, constitutional process a baseline constraint that enables presidential opportunities or forecloses them?

There is the danger of seeing contemporary events so closely in the rearview mirror as to magnify their importance as developmental milestones. We may be seeing the nuclear option Senate rules change out of proportion. Yet it would be myopic indeed not to notice the partisan-inflection of this institutional realignment in the advice and consent dynamic. The nuclear future may point to a zero-sum solution, in which presidents with party-compatible Senates max out their preferred judicial appointees while presidents without do without. Conversely, the nuclear future may simply assure that different times call for different kinds of nominees.

If the latter is the conclusion to draw, the options and the opportunities remain the president's to make. And the briefing book counsel to chief executives would be the same as it long has been: candidate qualifications are an elemental presidential calculation and an essential presidential compromise. The next chapter takes up this topic and this challenge.

TWO

CANDIDATES

"Excellence, diversity, and moderation"—these were the criteria one Democratic senator and member of the Senate Judiciary Committee advised President George W. Bush to look for, in his first opportunity to name a new Supreme Court justice (Eisgruber 2007, 178). The person ultimately nominated and confirmed, appointed in 2006 to fill retiring Justice Sandra Day O'Connor's seat, was federal judge Samuel Alito, who had a distinctly conservative background and voting record. Benefitting from a Republican-controlled Senate, Bush had the luxury of naming a candidate who need not hew to criteria listed by a minority party senator. As it happened, Alito was confirmed in a narrow and largely party-line vote of 58–42, with only four Democratic senators voting for and one Republican and an Independent voting against. Needless to say, the Democratic senator quoted above was not one of the four.

By 2014, and mid-way through President Obama's second term in office, a different Democratic senator and member of the Senate Judiciary Committee had this to say about court appointments: "the rawness and the starkness of the political clashes in the courts has highlighted the need to have people there that are of an ideological like mind" (Jeremy 2014). Bush would certainly have agreed with the principle, though likely not the specific like-mindedness this Democrat was urging.

Qualities and qualifications of candidates for the federal judiciary are the stuff of presidential nomination decisions. As the above episodes demonstrate, competing and at times conflicting criteria often present themselves. "Moderation" and "ideological like mind" seem mutually exclusive, with the former mostly signifying "not *your* ideological like mind." Accommodating either with "diversity" suggests that demographic factors might be preconditions to ideological ones. "Excellence," that chimera, hints at an "I know it when I see it" gold standard—unless an objective and agreed-upon measure of candidate merit exists. Of course, as a criterion for nominees it also begs the question, asked by Lee Epstein and Jeffrey Segal in their 2005 study *Advice and Consent*: why *would* presidents seek out meritorious candidates, especially since the Constitution does not require them to do so?

This second chapter focuses on the calculus of descriptive variables that a president must negotiate in selecting his judicial nominees. The emphasis in this chapter's discussion is on the political, legal, professional, personal, and demographic variables with respect to the *candidates* for nomination. As with the first chapter, the second chapter addresses the historical development of this variable matrix, explaining when and why certain variables rose to prominence in the presidential nomination equation. Presidential choices and their consequences, in terms of potential political costs or payoffs, are the structural motif of the chapter. Because presidential appointments to the US Supreme Court receive more high-level and public attention, these will dominate the chapter's scrutiny and assessment of presidential choices and their consequences.

A secondary message of this second chapter is how a president may use candidate qualifications to reduce informational uncertainty about the future on-the-bench performance of his/her prospective nominees. As recent research in political science shows, judicial candidates share the political values of their nominating president to a greater degree than ever before. The possibility of greater informational accuracy as to a candidate's political ideology heightens its importance in the nomination calculus. But though presidents by and large look for surrogates of themselves in deciding whom to nominate, other considerations affect whether a prospective appointee will successfully maximize a president's political influence on the federal judiciary. Those other considerations are whether a prospective candidate is likely to be successfully confirmed. Ideological like minds will only be certain and successful presidential surrogates if they find their way onto the bench. In order to reduce uncertainty about *that*, presidents cannot neglect the matrix of candidate qualifications that is in play in their own place and time.

Qualities versus Qualifications

There was never a detailed discussion at the Constitutional Convention in 1787 of the qualifications federal judges ought to have. Delegates repeatedly asserted that the qualities of character and fitness for the bench were requisite, but they disagreed strenuously as to which branch of government—executive or legislative—would best be able to evaluate them. As he did with so many things, Washington set the precedent for the presidential evaluative role within the Article II appointment power dynamic. He tended to select for his first Supreme Court nominees men he knew intimately, whose character and support for the Constitution's principles he could vouch for personally, and who had in fact been participants in the Constitutional Convention. Washington also began what would be a long tradition of naming candidates with prior judicial experience—in Washington's case, candidates who had served as jurists on high state courts. Finally, geographic representation was key: the diverse regional interests and state identities in the new nation influenced the mix of candidates Washington put forward for Senate confirmation. Washington established a reputation of trust in executive choices and proved by his performance that the executive branch was competent to evaluate potential judges.

That is not to say that he never bungled a choice; indeed, Washington's nominees also provide an early precedent of Senate rejection of a candidate's fitness to serve. This occurred in 1795, when the Senate refused to confirm John Rutledge as the second chief justice. Rutledge had been appointed as one of Washington's original Associate Justices, but had resigned before ever hearing a case. By the time of his renomination, his currency as a candidate had been altered by his outspoken objection to the

Jay Treaty, a cornerstone of Federalist diplomatic policy. There were also whisperings about his mental illness, or "insanity" as the usage of the time would have it. A Federalist majority of the Senate rejected his reconfirmation; subsequently, Rutledge would manifest serious and suicidal depression. His sad chapter affirmed the Senate's vital place in evaluating candidate quality. The Rutledge case also suggests more: not only that political or policy viewpoint qualifications mattered for judicial candidates, but that such qualifications could change or develop as a candidate matured in his political life—and that the Senate would evaluate on this basis, and not simply defer to the president.

In the early decades of the nineteenth century and before the parameters of senatorial courtesy became firmly established, there was variation in the criteria presidents used to select judicial appointees. "Certainly personal relationships, family ties, and party support came to influence presidents in choosing nominees. But presidents were also clearly considering potential judges' policy views," so Lee Epstein and Jeffrey Segal note in their *Advice and Dissent* (2005, 33). As far as ascertainable standards and criteria of ability go, a nominee's age, experience, and record in and out of public life were all available guidelines—with the latter also aiding a president in identifying those critical policy views. A candidate's geographic home base remained relevant as well and was the main demographic characteristic that a president weighed in making a selection for the Supreme Court. Geographic concerns of course played into the balance of interests among the members of the Senate, who deferred to one another's preferences with respect to judicial nominees for positions in their home states. But no Supreme Court nominee from a state whose home state senators refused their consent could prevail, either. Such was the informal rule and understood practice of senatorial courtesy. Yet geography was also a kind of a prior or limiting case for presidential nomination decisions: nineteenth century diversity on the high bench mandated a roughly proportional geographic distribution of justices. Geographic pressures also existed in the service of electoral goals, and a strategically chosen geographic-based appointment could pay dividends for a president and his party in terms of turning or repaying key states.

Partisan considerations are not always so instrumental, or even so (relatively) high-mindedly representative. Political favors and rewards—what might be crassly called cronyism—was and has been a feature of some presidents' nominations, to be sure. Still, this is an area in which a president must carefully calibrate other qualifications in the "crony" candidate's mix. There is of course the wise, if sour, adage of President Harry Truman that "whenever you put a man on the Supreme Court he ceases to be your friend." While friends' "real politics" can seemingly be known, friends cannot always be trusted to display them, it would also seem. Likewise, a pure patronage or payback nomination, without more, risks a needless showdown with a skeptical Senate. Presidents should thus attend to the lesson of "trust but verify": make sure that political allies also possess other redeeming or desirable qualities as candidates, as a form of assurance.

This brings us to the qualities of judicial temperament, ethics, and competence. Assurance qualities for sure, these criteria are sometimes called "the non-ideological smokescreen": issues employed to conceal the real reason for opposing a nominee (Massaro 1990, 8–9). A president who cuts corners on any one of them—especially when nominating a political favor or a personal friend—is likely to find any one of them the excuse in rejecting a crony or a patronage appointment. So merit, and meritorious candidates, matter because there is a threshold of satisfactoriness that must be cleared, and it is usually a composite of characteristics that clears it. Merit is in some ways less appreciable, less transparent than geographic background, or judicial experience, or even policy views. Still, as an intangible element, its absence is noted more than its presence is remarked or remarkable. Professional merit is understood to be there, in a president's choice . . . until it isn't.

Two examples showcase how deficiency in the merit qualities of judicial temperament, ethics, and competence can prevent a candidate's crossing that threshold of satisfactoriness. Nixon's "spite" nomination of Harrold Carswell in 1970 and

George W. Bush's selection of his personal attorney Harriet Miers in 2005 are similar in that each went down in defeat largely because of merit considerations. They are similar in few other ways, except that with each, the president had a point to make with his choice of candidate. That "point" was the raw exercise of presidential will, just as naked cronyism is a raw exertion of presidential power politics. The fact of the matter rendered each nominee suspect from the outset and susceptible to professional merit inquiry.

For Nixon, Carswell was something of a finger in the eye to the Senate, which had just refused to confirm his previous Supreme Court nominee Clement Haynsworth on ethics grounds. Nixon, it will be remembered from Chapter 1, had run on a campaign pledge to appoint strict constructionists to the court, to reverse the liberal activist trend of the Warren Court's decision making. He had also campaigned vigorously for electoral support in the South, from white conservatives. He wanted his appointee to fulfill those philosophical and geographic criteria. When Southern conservative jurist and native South Carolinian federal judge Haynsworth was rejected due to evidence of questionable financial practices and conflict-of-interest improprieties, Nixon quickly countered by nominating Carswell of Florida, a "little known and little distinguished" former federal district judge with a scant six months of service on the Fifth Circuit Court of Appeals. As Henry Abraham pointedly observes in *Justices, Presidents, and Senators,* "The appointment was an act of vengeance—one intended to teach the Senate a lesson and downgrade the court" (5th ed., p. 11). Carswell's glaring unsuitability/patent inferiority spanned White Supremacist statements to purposeful evasions of civil rights laws to one of the highest reversal (and thus higher court correction) rates of any sitting federal judge to alleged morals indiscretions that were, for the time, scandalous.[1] Nixon's point had been made, and the Senate went on to make its own in rejecting the president's second chosen candidate for the High Court. Unmoved doubtful senators had been, even by the pathetic and now-infamous appeal of Senator Hruska, the Republican floor manager of the nomination: "Even if he is mediocre there are a lot of mediocre judges and people and lawyers. They are entitled to a little representation, aren't they, and a little chance?"

Mediocrity in professional credentials was also on display in Bush's choice of Harriet Miers, whom he tapped to take the place of the first woman justice, Sandra Day O'Connor, who had announced her decision to retire once her successor could be named. Outright defiance of a coequal branch was not exactly the point Bush was making with his selection; "trust my judgment that she's one of us," comes closer to the mark. Miers was an old-fashioned crony candidate nominated for her personal loyalty to the president—but with the twist that the president could vouch for her ideological *bona fides.* "I know her heart," Bush asserted, as much to say *and that fact should be enough for anyone.* Sadly for him and more embarrassingly for her, it was not. Miers' debilities became woefully apparent as she proceeded through the questionnaires from the administration and the Judiciary Committee, on her jurisprudential views. Simply put, she was utterly lacking in constitutional knowledge or practical courtroom experience. Conservative Republicans in the Senate even began to doubt her reliability on abortion and other social issues, in that her intellectual legal resources seemed so thin. "Nominating a constitutional tabula rasa to sit on what is America's constitutional court," one conservative commentator fumed, "is an exercise of regal authority with the arbitrariness of a king giving his favorite general a particularly plush dukedom" (Quoted in Abraham, p. 320). Part of the problem was that Bush, like Nixon, had run on a platform to appoint justices who would narrowly construe the Constitution—who would, in essence, conform to a GOP-friendly interpretive approach on major legal policy issues. Bush's personal testimony that Miers would and could do so was insufficient to persuade even the president's erstwhile senatorial allies. Indeed, it, and the nomination itself, affronted and insulted them. Bare competence questions of merit undid the appointment of longtime Bush friend Miers, who withdrew her candidacy before her confirmation hearings even started, before her ranking by the ABA was even completed.

Professional merit evaluation has been, since 1956, largely in the hands of the ABA Standing Committee on Federal Judiciary. It is of course nowhere stated in the Constitution that a federal judge must be an attorney or even have a law degree. Nevertheless, convention now dictates both, with the major national bar association called upon to provide some objective measure of a nominee's standing as a legal professional. As the organization's literature details, evaluation is on the basis of these professional qualifications: integrity, professional competence, and judicial temperament. The standing committee uses information culled from a review of the nominee's legal experience, writing samples, and interviews with the nominee and members of the legal profession. From the last source, the ABA's committee discerns a candidate's general reputation in the legal community, which usually also speaks to temperament qualities such as "compassion, decisiveness, open-mindedness, courtesy, patience, and freedom from bias" (ABA Standing Committee webpage). Professional competence is closely tied to years of experience in the practice of law, particularly in-court trial work and in the judiciary; normally, twelve years is expected for an evaluation of "qualified" or "well qualified." Fewer years and less conventionally distinguished types of legal accomplishment could earn a nominee the devastating "non-qualified" rating.

Various disputes about the ABA's criteria of ranking arose. Democratic presidents such as Jimmy Carter and Bill Clinton, seeking to appoint diversity candidates who were women and racial minorities, found that these candidates' more limited or delayed opportunities for advancement automatically handicapped them in terms of the evaluation standards: women and African-Americans were by definition younger, relative newcomers to the legal and judicial professions compared to their white male counterparts. The committee subsequently modified its hard line on years of experience that had disadvantaged these groups. Conservative Republican presidents had other sorts of complaints with the ABA's approach to assessing professional qualifications. Reagan and both Bushes sought to appoint younger and younger judges who would serve for a long time, as well as legal academics with sharply defined jurisprudential positions; both qualities would help maximize presidential influence on the composition and decision making of the federal bench. But both qualities tested the parameters of merit: younger jurists had fewer years of professional service and sometimes also lacked the traditional kinds of legal experience that the ABA valued. Age had, of course, always been a nomination consideration for presidents: a nominee who was too elderly and potentially too infirm to serve for long was deemed disqualified, but appointees of an appropriately "seasoned" age had likewise been an expectation. These days, youth, far from being a demerit, is practically a requisite for smart presidential selections. Democratic President Obama followed in the footsteps of his Republican predecessors in seeking relatively young appointees with many years on the bench before them.

Merit factors are hardly neutral, but in the current appointment climate, merit cleaves strongly to practical legal experience, particularly prior judicial experience. So while not identical to merit, which partakes of other ability and integrity qualities, experience (particularly prior judicial, for Supreme Court-level nominees) has been deployed by recent presidents as a kind of guarantee of candidate merit. Presidents, moreover, are expected to provide it in their youngest, seemingly most accelerated appointees.

If merit and experience tend to conflate, merit and credentialing also tend to produce a fairly homogenous group of Supreme Court justices. Law degrees from the most prestige law schools, particularly Harvard and Yale, dominate on the contemporary high bench and suggest a uniformly elite educational experience. This, combined with the prevalence of appointees with lower federal court and especially appellate court experience, yields a judicial group with a somewhat narrow set of professional encounters and a lack of contact with the world of practical policy making. What impact this has on their decision making is unclear. That presidents have difficulty bucking this trend is clear and will be discussed in the next section.

The matter of merit qualifications and pressures to conform to expected ones brings up a last pairing, that of merit and diversity. Merit and diversity have a similar intertwined relationship to those selection criteria mentioned above. Where standards of merit and qualities of demographic diversity were once thought of as distinct or even in tension, diversity is increasingly seen as a kind of merit consideration, with a candidate of an under- or unrepresented identity bringing a needed alternative viewpoint on the law, or simply introducing the diversity variable into the collegial deliberation process and thus potentially affecting organizational behavior. This contemporary stance on diversity as a quality is a bit different than the way demographic difference originally functioned in the appointment calculus. Demographic representation on the federal bench was of course once limited to considerations of geography, as the nominee pool contained only white male Protestant candidates. A geographically representative nominee provided not only a descriptive but also a symbolic kind of representation that could be used for electoral outreach purposes. As the demographic criteria expanded beyond geographic place, the representational equation remained the same. Religion was the first threshold that was crossed, with Catholic appointees followed by the first Jewish appointee to the Supreme Court in 1916. These, and ethnic nominees, such as Irish in the nineteenth and other "white ethnics" in the twentieth century, Hispanic in the twentieth and twenty-first centuries, ensured that the courts "looked like America" but also appealed to blocs of same-ethnic group voters. Race and African-American and Asian-American, and gender and women appointees have played a similar role, in integrating the court and also serving parties' electoral objectives with respect to recruiting racial minority and female voters. Gays and lesbians, in the age in which attitudes toward same-sex marriage are rapidly liberalizing, are the latest demographic diversity appointees. Yet these Obama administration appointments are, interestingly, less about seeking LGBT individuals' votes for a particular political party than they are about demonstrating the party's policy position on discrimination and personal liberty issues to the younger generational bloc in the electorate.

Demographic considerations can also be political and electoral ones, and a demographically diverse bench can be of symbolic value as well as evidence of merit considerations in selecting judicial candidates—with merit here meaning a life experience of difference and challenge contributing to a new and different and *needed* viewpoint on the law. Of course, a link between identity—ethnic, religious, racial, gender-based, class-based—and experience *and resultant legal policy views* can never be far from the presidential mind. The life of the law is not logic but experience, Justice Oliver Wendall Holmes famously remarked. The law of judicial appointment is not politics but *identity* politics, the modern chief executive might well retort.

Criteria, Choices, and Consequences

Presidents, for sure, seek those diversity candidates whose experiences, personal and professional, align them with presidential ideology. Presidents also expect to receive credit for their "famous first" appointees. Lyndon Johnson's appointment of Thurgood Marshall in 1967 as the first African-American on the Supreme Court, Ronald Reagan's selection of Sandra Day O'Connor as the first woman justice in 1981, and Barack Obama's pick of the "wise Latina" Sonia Sotomayor in 2009 redounded to the benefit of the president in question, reputation-wise. Whether each appointment did so with respect to the electoral fortunes of the president's party is more difficult to discern. But the received wisdom is that demographic or diversity factors, particularly in regard to racial and ethnic identity, pay political dividends in (1) rewarding and solidifying a faithful constituency (Johnson, Democrats, and black voters but also white/Jewish liberals), (2) remedying or closing an appreciable deficiency in the party's electorate (Reagan, Republicans, and the "gender gap" among women voters), or (3) appealing for the loyalty and support of an uncommitted or wavering group of voters (Obama, Democrats, and Hispanics—although George W. Bush perhaps deserves credit for the intention and faltering attempt to nominate his Attorney General Alberto Gonzales in 2005).

A president also has his or her legacy to think of, and this is measured not only in the fluctuating currency of reputation in history, but in the cold hard cash of policy impact on the federal judiciary. Both the number of candidates placed, overall, and the influential nature of individual appointees matter. Raw numbers translate into the ability for one's partisans to dominate three-judge circuit panels or *en banc* majorities of the federal courts of appeal; appointees' influence can come via their sheer intellectual star power or their strategic situation as a critical swing justice. Judicial nominations are a tool, and tools can be wielded skillfully or ineptly. The trick is for a president to master the linkage between criteria, choices on their basis, and consequences of those choices.

As the previous section suggested, the criteria on which candidates are selected has varied over time. Still, certain patterns and consistencies exist. While some presidents prioritize judicial staffing over other items in the presidential agenda, all presidents (should) care about candidate ideology. What varies is how much a president stresses it, and stresses it as against other selection criteria. A rule of thumb—which will be developed more completely in the next chapter on the context of confirmation—is that as presidential political capital decreases, so must the proportional emphasis on the nominee's "fit" with the president's policy views and/or constitutional vision. Presidents in weakened or straightened circumstances must name composite candidates: potential appointees with compelling qualities of merit qualifications and/or demographic diversity that neutralize or balance out or, at times, supersede partisanship or political ideology. This fact has not changed; only the recipe for the composite has.

One pattern in the criteria for judicial candidates that is clearly apparent is the development of greater precision in what is meant by professional merit. Legal acumen and legal experience—as understood and vetted by the major national bar association—is the categorical standard. A certain number of years of federal courtroom practice does not guarantee smooth confirmation, but it dispels quality questions. The ABA, moreover, has broadened its definition of the kinds of legal practice in which excellence is valued. Recall that the Brandeis nomination was noteworthy in demonstrating the new Progressive era notion of professional and especially legal merit: impactful legal advocacy. Experience as an advocate, particularly of public interest law, also figured in the appointments of Thurgood Marshall and Ruth Bader Ginsburg, whose legal careers with the NAACP Legal Defense Fund and the ACLU's Women's Rights Project, respectively, were merit qualifications attributes, to be sure. But this professional experience was even more a signal as to the ideological leanings of each nominee. And the professional dossier of each was further leavened by service as solicitor general and federal appellate court judge, respectively. These most elite levels of legal experience are almost requisite for contemporary Supreme Court nominees—such that the appointees to each office are considered the presidential "farm team" for the high court.

Professional merit with respect to educational merit shows a constrictive kind of precision. As has been observed, there is a Harvard-Yale JD stranglehold on the current membership of the Supreme Court. (Indeed, this kind of "degree elitism" extends to the Supreme Court law clerks—who are, themselves, a pool from which future judicial nominees are drawn.) The skewedness of the legal educational experience toward the Ivy League, combined with the prevalence of justices with lower federal court and especially federal appellate court experience, yields a judicial group with a somewhat narrow set of personal and professional encounters and a lack of contact with the world of practical policy making. Even presidents that desire to do so have difficulty bucking this trend. Off-brand candidates for the Supreme Court—Bill Clinton's and George W. Bush's politicians with "big hearts," for instance—are really relics of another era, an era of senators expressing deference to the expertise of their senatorial colleagues, for instance. President Obama never really seriously considered such an appointee, although some commentators speculate that he would like to be considered as one himself. How his political experience and obvious partisanship would figure in the assessment of his merit qualifications by opposition-party senators is not difficult to predict; what is more interesting to ask is whether a future Democrat in the White House could make a successful "institutional diversity viewpoint" case for the nomination of this former chief executive.

This brings us to another pattern we can discern in the selection of judicial nominees: how the definition of the "demographic" diversity criterion develops. It is, quite frankly, tied to the expansion of the electorate and of political equality in general, as new interests and groups are accommodated into political life and thus into the dynamics of party politics. This pattern explains the racial, ethnic, and gender demographics of the current Supreme Court. Similarly, the court's patently non-diverse religious and regional demographics (Roman Catholics and New Yorkers are quite overrepresented, proportionally speaking) indicate the lack of electoral relevance of these diversity criteria (although the Muslim religious identity may be a diversity consideration for the future). It is to demographic groups active in electoral politics and actively courted by the parties-in-the-electorate that demographic diversity-oriented judicial appointments are directed. While this developmental pattern is relatively obvious, the timing of the selection of such diversity appointees is not. Its urgency is contingent.

For diversity criteria, that contingency is a matter of availability and opportunity, plus a smattering of personal presidential priority. Consistency, on the other hand, is found in presidential utilization of the ideological criterion for selection of judicial candidates. Still, *how* a president goes about identifying ideologically attractive nominees has become a more sophisticated and, arguably, scientific operation. This is true whether a president and his/her White House team are assembling a politically plausible or confirmable composite template or scanning the horizon for an intellectual superstar of the left or right. More staff time and attention to sifting and screening, more data as to previous writings and judicial voting records, and more assiduous questionnaire completion and personal interviews done by prospective candidates—all this yields a more fine-tuned ability to carefully plot an appointee's performance in confirmation and on the bench.

The Uncertainty Factor

Presidents who have upped the ante on nominating correctly have done so by minimizing the uncertainty factor in their judicial appointees. This is part of the reason for the increasing standardization of the quality of professional merit or what used to be known simply as a candidate's "qualifications." When all parties—political and institutional—are forced to agree as to the standard of a highly qualified nominee, it cannot be a point of attack or a vulnerability. Similarly, when diversity becomes not simply electoral payoff or payback but "diversity of viewpoint" (an expected one, and on policy views, to be sure) and thus a legitimate qualification, the demographic representation criterion loses its stigma of "tokenism." Unpredictable factors become predictable, positive ones.

Potentially, the only nonideological quality that retains its sting, in terms of contaminating a nominee, is being a political ally or friend. But the tutorial here—lame-duck president Lyndon Johnson and his fateful effort to elevate sitting justice and long-time confidante Abe Fortas to the chief justice chair—speaks more to timing and circumstance than substance. This episode's generation of the so-called "Thurmond rule" for Senate action on judicial nominations in the final six months of a presidential term will be further explored in the next chapter, on the politico-institutional context of presidential judicial appointments. Johnson's own inability to assess his diminished political clout aside, it could be argued that Obama's 2010 naming of his very brand-new Solicitor General Elena Kagan to the Supreme Court was as a party-regular and White House team player and that George W. Bush proved (more than once) that cronyism never really went out of style. Nevertheless, the kind of unpleasant surprises that Johnson faced regarding Fortas' damning financial escapades, or that Bush encountered with respect to Miers' professional stature, are much less likely to occur, as are such debilities on the part of political friends much less likely to be overlooked. Presidential selection of federal judges has been almost thoroughly professionalized, leaving little room for favors or favoritism. This is not to say that "friends with benefits" do not end up on the federal bench—only that those benefits must include sterling and predictably assessed credentials, in addition to trustworthy policy views.

The last refuge of unpredictable judicial nominations is nominee performance at the confirmation hearing. The presidential fear is of the unguarded remark, the philosophical revelation that sinks the appointment. Until the quite recent publication of two studies of candidate candor at Senate confirmation hearings since 1955, the conventional wisdom was that nominee outspokenness has been in precipitous decline ever since Robert Bork's testimonial tour de force ended his Supreme Court prospects. Nominees, it was thought, had instilled (or had had instilled in them) the lesson to speak in soaring and dismissive generalities and, more to the point, to decline to answer questions about cases or issues likely to come before them—out of an excess of judicial modesty, presumably. This "Ginsburg rule" is so called for the unforthcoming responses supplied by Ruth Bader Ginsburg during her questioning by the Senate Judiciary Committee in 1993. As Dion Farganis and Justin Wedeking characterize it in their 2014 book *Supreme Court Confirmation Hearings in the U.S. Senate: Reconsidering the Charade*, "Her self-imposed policy against providing 'previews' or 'forecasts' . . . is synonymous with the kind of obfuscation that has saddled the hearings with the bad reputation they have today" (p. 46). Still, to the extent that this practice is a regularity, it makes confirmation proceedings predictable and predictably unrevealing and—from a presidential perspective—nonthreatening.

The problem with the Ginsburg rule is that, as a rule, it is patently false. Post-Bork Supreme Court nominees have been no more evasive than their predecessors, nor were earlier nominees wellsprings of responsiveness and their hearings exercises in openness and substance. There has been little variation in hearings questioning and content over time and less outright "evasion" than is commonly thought. Indeed, the second recent study of nominee testimony argues that the hearings are substantively valuable in expressing and solidifying the areas of law and policy that are settled and that candidates "repeatedly affirm their allegiance to (or rejection of) what were once disputed constitutional meanings" (Collins and Ringhand 2013, 7). This empirically informed evaluation of nominees in the confirmation process is at once worrisome and comforting to the modern chief executive. Comforting because the affirmation of seminal cases, like *Brown v. Board of Education*, is a catechism any well-schooled candidate can perform, but worrisome because (opposition) senators should be expected to constantly and persistently test the waters as to "the constitutional issues that are and are not actively in play" (p. 8).

The lesson here, for presidents and their judicial nominees, is that preparation matters. Knowing in advance where a prospective appointee's previous statements or writings reveal something troubling, something precipitating examination, allows the president and his judicial selection team to anticipate and advise. Planning for the confirmation proceedings, extending to the use of mock hearings questioning, is how a president sees his nominations through. But some raw material can be worked with; some cannot. Predicting *this* is the elemental presidential calculation of nominee qualities and qualifications, by nominating someone who knows which constitutional policy issues are not contested and furthermore knows how to speak about those that are. Put another way, nominating someone who knows when to present certainty and when to express—but not necessarily adhere to—uncertainty.

Note

1. While not revealed in his FBI report, during further investigations into Carswell's background, his affairs with men while he was married came to light. This was troublesome, commented John Dean, Nixon's White House counsel, who continued wryly: "while Richard Nixon was always looking for historic firsts, nominating a homosexual to the high Court would not have been on his list" (Epstein and Segal 2005, 70).

THREE

CONTEXT

The Democratic bloodbath that was the 2014 midterm election guaranteed that the final two years of President Obama's second term would be a difficult one, judicial appointments-wise. The Republican recapture of a comfortable majority in the US Senate portended a senatorial role of "advice and dissent." As a 2009 study by the same name observes, judicial selection is "a set of inherited institutional practices that have evolved over time" with presidents and Senate majorities having to "grapple with the broad and increasingly interconnected array of procedural rights that shape the fate of nominees before the Senate" (Binder and Maltzman 2009, 145–6). This institutional setting and the partisan interests that are mapped onto it together constitute the context within which a president must work to secure successful confirmation of his or her judicial candidates for office.

The previous chapter examined the criteria presidents use in choosing their judicial nominees, pairing choices made on the basis of certain criteria with the consequences presidents can expect from making them. The emphasis was on the potential electoral consequences of choosing certain candidates, but the chapter also considered the way in which certain candidate qualities can reduce informational uncertainty about what those prospective candidates will experience in confirmation proceedings. This chapter continues that exploration, shifting the focus from the candidates' qualities to the institutional context and political climate in which those candidates are assessed. The message of this third chapter is how a president should understand and navigate these in order to reduce "political uncertainty" as to the confirmation prospects of putative appointees.

The previous chapter concluded with some observations about the value of preparing nominees for the confirmation hearing experience. In this chapter, the attention turns to the full battery of separation of powers dynamics that structure the Article III appointment power. Here, too, the scope of analysis widens to encompass staffing of the entire federal judiciary, from Supreme Court to circuit to district court levels. The conditions that inform a president's strategic calculation of his best strategic actions will be detailed, from party control of the Senate to presidential political capital to the number and kind of judicial vacancies that exist. Both presidential procedural options and senatorial procedural machinations—including, most importantly, those with obstructionist potential—will be described and evaluated for their significance in affecting the confirmation process. Finally, the increasingly *less* ancillary and *less* sporadic role of interest group participation in the process will be discussed, as this impacts both senatorial and Judiciary Committee behavior and public opinion responses to the president's prospective judges.

The President and the Strategic Approach to Judicial Appointment: A Prologue

Strategic action is about understanding the institutional setting in which decision making occurs. The institutional setting is the structure of procedural or rule-based powers and constraints, with judicial appointment the product of interdependent choices of the presidential and senatorial actors within this structure of interactions. But it is the political preferences and motivations of those actors that bring those institutional interactions and interdependent choices to life. A president acts strategically when he or she realizes that the success or failure of his or her judicial appointments depends on the preferences of other actors and the actions he or she expects them to take.

Key to a president's strategic calculation is awareness of what might be called Senate "veto points." Veto points are moments when procedural options can be exercised that stall, thwart, or terminate the decision process—the process, in other words, of deciding on the confirmation of a judicial candidate. These veto points will be carefully described in a subsequent section of this chapter; for now, suffice it to say that such procedural vetoes may or may not be exercised: some decisions to do or not do so a president can influence, some he or she cannot. A president should assume that there are multiple pivotal points in the Senate—some potentially competing—at which a nominee could be blocked from being confirmed. Generally speaking, the more partisan opposition the Senate, the more veto points are armed and ready. But even a Senate minority, and even a determined single senator, can limit a president's room to maneuver, in terms of naming appointees who are close political or ideological affiliates and are thus more likely to garner unwanted attention and/or energized resistance. In order to proceed through the confirmation process, the president's judicial selections must take into account when Senate actors will be motivated and mobilized to succeed in opposing his or her choices. Sometimes partisanship dictates these motivations and mobilization, sometimes the political calendar does. These political conditions are the subtext to the institutional powers and constraints that make up the judicial appointment process and are the subject of the next section of this chapter.

Before moving to that subject, however, there is one other factor to mention with implications for senatorial use of its procedural vetoes: the institutional culture of the Senate. At one time, protocol, custom, and convention[1] could be counted on to discourage senatorial challenge to judicial nominees—as, for example, when senators of both parties routinely deferred to the appointments prerogative of the newly elected president, out of acceptance of the norm that "elections have consequences." As Democrat Rep. Rahm Emanuel was reported as saying, as recently as 2006, to his congressional colleagues and partisans: "George Bush won the election. If you don't like it, you better win elections" (Quoted in Silverstein 2007, 224). Still, the operative influence of protocol, custom, and convention on senatorial behavior is lessening, such that few norms of comity can be relied upon to restrain senators from constraining presidential judicial selection. Testifying to this is the reaction from Republican Senate Judiciary Committee member Jeff Sessions, to Barack Obama's first appellate court nomination in 2009. Decrying the selection of this nominee, the senator blustered, "I believe the president deserves deference, but he's about used all the deference he's going to get out of me" (Quoted in Binder and Maltzman 2009, 103).

Conversely, some customs have force and actually activate senatorial obstruction. There is, for example, the practice of vacancy hoarding in presidential election years, with opposition-party senators driving their institution to a moratorium on any new confirmations of the sitting president's judicial nominees. The cutoff point is somewhat imprecise, hovering somewhere around the final six months of a president's last year of term. This unofficially recognized "Thurmond Rule" is named for the conservative Southern Senator Strom Thurmond, for his opposition to the end-of-term Supreme Court nominations of lame-duck President Lyndon Johnson. Declining to run for reelection in 1968 amid the escalating difficulties of the Vietnam War, Johnson in the summer of his final year in office and with a Republican increasingly likely as his successor sought to secure the appointment of his friend and political associate and sitting associate justice Abe Fortas to the Chief Justiceship. Fortas' candidacy soon became awash in controversies of its own, connected to allegations about financial conflict of interest and related improprieties. Johnson also committed several serious errors in presidential management of the nomination, particularly in his dealings with key Senate allies. His nominee to replace the associate justiceship to be made vacant by Fortas' elevation raised further hackles, politically speaking. Ultimately and somewhat in retrospect, Senate opponents coalesced around the position that to confirm what amounted to two strongly partisan appointments by an outgoing liberal Democratic president would be an abdication of advice and consent power and an inappropriate concession of the Senate's coequal role in shaping the federal judiciary. The decision not to move on lifetime judicial appointments as a president is ending his or her term in office emerged as an informal and somewhat amorphous "rule" that is dismissed when politically inconvenient and so inconsistently applied when it is applied at all. Yet despite its lack of universal acceptance, this institutional custom or practice *can be* brought to bear on the appointment process. The upshot is that presidents need to be aware of all this, as part of appreciating the institutional setting and interdependent choice environment in which they are acting.

The somewhat whimsical nature of Senate obeisance to norm and custom aside, presidents nevertheless can affect the senatorial decision whether to actuate its various veto points: by presenting their judicial candidates in such a way as to increase the senatorial costs—political and/or institutional—of opposing them. Timing, "bundling," and packaging of federal judicial nominees constitute the procedural stratagems presidents can employ to maximize candidate confirmation, whatever the political environment.

Political Conditions and Presidential Strategic Action

The contemporary climate of partisan polarization has definitively changed the Senate confirmation dynamic, as the Senate's record in confirming judicial nominees over the past six decades aptly illustrates. That record is one of a declining rate of and an increasing time till confirmation. As Binder and Maltzman explain in their *Advice and Dissent*, in recent years the two political parties "have taken their battles down to a micro-level, carefully targeting individual [circuit] courts depending on the ideological tenor of the bench. Such strategies by the parties complicate presidents' efforts to reshape the bench as they see fit, even when their party controls both the White House and the Senate" (2009, 84).

Against the bracing reality of this political climate, presidents also must evaluate specific political conditions that vary and are thus contingencies informing a president's strategic calculation of his best course of action. Again, those choices of action concern the timing, bundling, and packaging of federal judicial nominees. When is it appropriate versus inappropriate to try to push and/or rush through judicial nominees? When is it advisable if not requisite to bundle nominations as a slate of judicial candidates? What kind of packaging and promotion of nominees is necessary in certain situations? Time and effort must be expended on judicial appointment; time and resources are always limited and must be husbanded and efficiently distributed to items within the presidential agenda. Time and resources are also preferentially distributed to items within a particular presidential agenda. Calculating that preference and its priority—whether and how much to devote in the judicial staffing context—is what presidential strategic action is all about. Ultimately, then, the best use of time and energy in the appointment context is directly determined by the value of variables specific to the presidential political situation.

These variables are (1) party control of the Senate, (2) presidential political capital, and (3) status quo of the federal judiciary including number of vacancies and balance of power vacancies that exist/occur. These variables interact as factors to create the presidential political situation and the probability of Senate cooperation in the executive project of judicial staffing. Their possible values are (1) same- versus opposition-party majority, filibuster "proof" (supra) versus non-filibuster proof majority, and variation as to the ideologically median senator in the committee versus the full Senate; (2) electoral mandate and approval rating, as well as point in presidential term; and (3) size of the vacancy backlog and the existence of vacancy "emergencies," as well as strategic vacancies that alter the partisan balance of power on a court/composition of appellate court panels. Simply put, the state of judicial vacancies affects calculation as to the prioritizing of judicial staffing in the presidential agenda, all other things being equal.

Clearly, the party composition of the Senate is the "thing" of paramount importance to a president in calculating the successful confirmation of his or her judicial candidates. With a friendly Senate comes a same-party-controlled Judiciary Committee, although not all partisan allies are created equal. Differences across the conservative–liberal dimension within the president's own political party can affect the willingness of same-party senators to move expeditiously on their chief executive's nominees. The same dimensional range also affects the senators from the opposition party, although the presence of moderate centrists in the Senate from either party has been steadily diminishing over the last two decades. Still, the so-called Senate "medians" exist in the full Senate and on the Judiciary Committee, but these may not and in fact usually are not the same people. The upshot is that a president may be dealing with a committee that is substantially more adverse, ideologically speaking, than its Senate, or vice versa, and this dynamic applies to same-party- and opposition-party-controlled bodies. Median senators matter because they are the pivot points for creating majoritarian voting coalitions in their respective committee or chamber. Clearly, ideological and other political differences between these respective median senators require altered presidential negotiation tactics and a custom-fitting of a president's appeals regarding his or her nominees to the committee versus the full Senate majority.

Generally speaking, presidents should capitalize on periods of same-party control of the body to put forth candidates for available vacancies. Both first and second term presidents should remember that midterm elections are times when voters ratify the president's performance; such elections can present opportunities for the opposition party to shift the balance of power within Congress and can be occasions when a president's party loses seats and may even lose a party majority in the Senate. Seniority rules for committee leadership will then dictate a change in the party and the person of the chair of the critically important Senate Judiciary Committee. Even if the president's party does not lose control of the Senate, its margin of control can be greatly diminished—liquidating a supra-majority margin and cushion and maximizing the influence of median senators who may be only sometime ideological allies. Aside from allowing the shedding of such fair-weather partisan friends and still constituting a majority to confirm, supra-majorities can be so large as to subvert the senatorial veto tactic of the filibuster. This Senate procedure allows a minority to hold up Senate business, including moving to a floor vote on a judicial nominee, by extending debate. A 3/5 majority or 60 of 100 senators must be assembled to evoke cloture and override this dilatory tactic of incessant talking. Famous examples of filibustering bills have included senators taking the podium to read from the phone book and holding the floor in continuous "debate" for periods approaching twenty-four hours. Filibustering is more than just a bother, it can be an effective roadblock, particularly by a determined and concerted group of minority party senators. Even the threat of the filibuster can be enough to keep a nominated candidate in limbo, as Senate leaders of the president's party attempt to bargain with or otherwise wait out their colleagues' objections.

Timing, bundling, and packaging all come into play here. A president is advised not to waste or squander time, when he or she has an advantageous same-party Senate to work with. Do not putter, and defer. Bundling of nominees—putting forth a slate of several lower court nominees, as a group—is another method of taking advantage of fortuitous circumstances and "catching up" on extant vacancies. This is particularly true at the beginning of a new president's term in office, when vacancy hoarding at the end of the previous administration may have left a sizeable backlog of appointments to make. Of course, some presidents have the great bad fortune to inherit only a few judicial appointment opportunities upon taking office. "Midnight" or late-in-term court packing by an outgoing occupant of the other party, or even succeeding an especially successful party fellow, can leave an incoming president with little judicial staffing to do and little immediate benefit to reap from a friendly Senate. This is a time for the preparation of a list of prospective, desirable judicial candidates who may be proposed, separately or together, in the future. As to the latter, presenting candidates as a group, it is "a strategy for all seasons." Bundling is a way of taking the spotlight off of any one particular candidate, and his or her perhaps contentious ideological profile, in favor of presenting a more-or-less heterogeneous mix of judicial nominees, reflecting a broad range of candidate qualities. Bundling becomes even more important as the size of the same-party majority diminishes and as the size and ideological polarity of the party opposition increases. Likewise, packaging of nominees—framing and presenting them in terms of their best and most broadly acceptable qualifications—is most important to convince reluctant senators and, in particular, to convince them that opposition to a particular nominee or nominees is not ultimately worth their while because reframing a nominee in an alternate and negative way is not (or not very) possible. Reluctant senators are most often found in the opposition party, but not always. Putative Senate allies, particularly those on the Judiciary Committee or representing a state housing the judicial vacancy, will also expect to be accommodated. Proper packaging can demonstrate that this has been done.

With respect to party control of the Senate as a variable in the political conditions mix, its influence varies somewhat with respect to Supreme Court, court of appeals, and district court appointment opportunities. So too do the corresponding tactical actions available to a president, in moving prospective justices versus lower federal court judges through to confirmation. Except in extreme situations, there is no bundling of Supreme Court appointees, simply because the probability of multiple vacancies is low. Timed—let alone timed and coordinated—retirements from the court, as a form of payback to a president and/or his or her party, are never guaranteed. Nor are Supreme Court retirements to be regularly expected, in the course of some natural institutional attrition. Recall Jimmy Carter, who served his entire presidential term without a single high court vacancy to fill. Supreme Court justices are free agents, who are under no compunction to create or "return" an available seat. Moreover, as judges at the pinnacle of the judicial career, many prefer to remain until the functional end of that career—stubbornly hanging on and thwarting a president's ambition to name his or her "own" justice. Timing of these nominations is thus seldom in a president's hands.

Although Supreme Court vacancies are not completely serendipitous (i.e., a feature of mortality alone), they can materialize or fail to, unexpectedly, and even inconveniently. If one does occur during a time of opposition-party control, packaging of the president's replacement candidate is essential. The worst-case scenario is a nominee released to the confirmation process without proper preparation—both of the nominee himself or herself and as to the nominee and his or her "story." Even in times of same-party Senate control, all senators will be critically engaged in the process of appointing a new Supreme Court justice, and minority party senators can burden an appointee's progress through the process, even if they cannot fully impede it. Stratagems and practices such as the filibuster come into play here, as will be further explored in the next section of this chapter. What is important to note in this context is that the size of a same-party Senate majority matters, in that a supra-majority, operating with party discipline and presidential supportiveness, virtually defangs most forms of senatorial obstruction of a president's choice of justice.

With respect to presidential choices for lower federal courts, it used to be the case that the Senate paid them less careful scrutiny; this is no longer quite true. Still, given the routinely larger number of such judicial openings and the reality of the functional necessity of keeping up with them, a president can expect some Senate cooperation in staffing these workhorse courts of the federal judiciary—even from a Senate controlled by the opposition. In the context of lower federal court appointees, the Senate's attention—particularly an opposite-party-controlled Senate's attention—shifts to the overall number of vacancies and alteration in partisan balance in the composition of particular circuits and across the lower federal courts as a whole. This is where opposition senators/opposition senates direct their energies: on maintaining parity or preserving their party's advantage in terms of the number of judges named. At times, such energies mitigate against cooperative efforts to fully or even reasonably resupply the intermediate appellate and trial-level federal courts. In addition, opposition senators/opposition senates are loathe to allow a president to equip a "farm team" for the US Supreme Court, by salting the federal appellate courts with credible contenders—or contenders made more credible, by virtue of being once confirmed as federal judges—for elevation to the high bench.

Despite the vagaries of Senate cooperation, presidents are expected to demonstrate cooperativeness with senators in certain appointment contexts, irrespective of which party controls the body. For instance, for all lower federal court appointments a president must at least go through the motions of considering the specific wishes of home state senators with respect to "their" federal judges. This is particularly the case at the level of district court candidates, whose jurisdiction is wholly contained within a single state's boundaries. In addition, appointments to federal circuit courts are expected to be roughly proportional to the states contained within their jurisdiction, giving particular states' senators rotating claims to influence the replacement for certain seats. The reason for a president to manifest such executive spirit of inter-branch teamwork is that home state members of the Senate have a particular veto point option in such situations. Known as the "blue slip" custom, this aspect of senatorial courtesy gives the two senators from the state in which the district or relevant circuit court appointment resides the option to withhold their consent to it, thus negating—or, at least, potentially impeding—any further action on the prospective appointee. While the strictures of this practice have varied over time and are not as ironclad as they once were, the blue slip has been a Senate prerogative extended to senators of either political party. It is, thus, an executive courtesy as well, extended to the Senate as a body and to the president's senatorial partisans in particular. As Mitchel Sollenberger explains in his 2003 summary for the Congressional Research Service, "it is enormously damaging to a senator's prestige if a president of his own party ignores him when it comes to making an appointment from or to the senator's own state. What is even more damaging to a senator's prestige and political power is for the president to appoint to high federal office someone who is known back home as a political opponent to the senator." While these days it is the home state senator(s) from the president's own party whose assent truly matters and whose objections are taken to be critical, presidents are still expected to engage in some prenomination consultation with all home state senators, partisan opponents included—lest the latter's displeasure with a lower federal court nominee becomes an excuse and a vehicle for senatorial resistance.

Senatorial "courtesy vetoes" like the blue slip practice depend for their efficacy on the Senate's institutional support for them, as embodied in the Senate party leadership. Presidents of course know this and know with whom they are working, in the persons of the Senate Majority Leader and the Chair of the Senate Judiciary Committee. But individual senators of a variety of stripes, from Judiciary Committee members to lone ideological firebrands, have their own veto point options known as "holds." These procedural maneuvers and their varying credibility will be discussed more fully in the next section, but the reality of their existence—and of their exercise by majority or minority party member—requires a president to be mindful of negotiation opportunities with Senate party leaders, and these of course differ in same-party- versus opposition-party-controlled senates. Blue slipping and other such vetoes can be trumped, or disregarded entirely, but it requires a vigorously motivated Judiciary Committee chair to do so. Such motivation can come from various sources, including changed senatorial norms of reciprocity and respect. But in terms of a committee chair or majority leader being motivated to discount an individual senator's objection to a judicial candidate—being motivated, in other words, not to exercise the discretion to slow down consideration of the candidate—there is no substitute for being a presidential sympathizer and ideological ally.

How party matters, then, is that party is not the whole story, when it comes to presidential strategic calculation of his or her best course of action, appointment-wise. Party control of the Senate naturally interacts with presidential political capital, the second political condition affecting the context of the judicial appointment process. Popular presidents with an electoral mandate are almost always presidents who enjoy same-party senatorial control and support. But presidential political capital is more than just presidential popularity: both presidents and their agendas have a shelf life. For a president, his political capital expiration date is closely connected to the viability of his or her coattails as a candidate or a party symbol at the top of the ticket, electorally speaking. Call it instrumental popularity. What it means is that a president who is not or cannot be seeking reelection, and who has no remaining persuasive clout with voters, should assume that his or her ability to secure confirmation of preferred judicial candidates is at its nadir. The *only* advantage, at this point, can come from the partisan makeup of the Senate and its collective willingness to continue to restock the federal courts with presiding judges.

For a president's agenda, its expiration date depends on how much time, bargaining, and rhetoricizing the president has devoted to its various issues. Agenda issues on which a president has little to show may have nevertheless sapped that president's reservoir of confidence, from the public, his or her party colleagues, his or her legislative branch partners. Even issues on which a president has been successful, in terms of securing legislation or budget allocation or judicial personnel, drain the agenda's capital reserves. The president's political capital is greatest in the honeymoon period of his or her initial term, can be renewed by landslide reelection and confirmatory midterm election results, but to use it is to lose it. Failing a subsequent popular acclamation and reaffirmation, or a national crisis that spurs a "rally 'round the flag/the chief executive" syndrome on Capitol Hill, a president's agenda can only become depleted and stale.

As political capital declines with time in office and nearness to lame-duckism, or is spent on presidential projects and not replenished, a president must adjust his or her judicial appointment strategies. For some presidents, either given their circumstances (optimal vacancies) or predilections (commitment to legal policy issues), staffing the federal courts is the highest priority in the presidential domestic agenda. Such presidents move quickly and with alacrity, bundle prodigiously, and aggressively and preemptively package their nominees, making the most of the moment when their popularity and political persuasiveness is at its apex. But the time (in terms of both duration and opportunistic earliness), effort, and resources devoted to the judicial agenda item are therefore diverted from other agenda items whose accomplishment may be important for a president's short-term political future or longer term political reputation. Certainly, a president and his or her partisans can credit claim in their campaigns and run on a successful series of appointments or a wholesale remaking of the federal judiciary; the capital so spent can produce dividends electorally and thus be regenerating. But normally, a president must economize and make hard choices as to how to allocate his energies. Efficient expenditures are preferable. Limits are finite.

And some causes are lost. No amount of bundling or packaging of judicial nominees can compensate for a Senate controlled by one's political enemies and a dwindling amount of presidential influence. Just as Johnson was forced to accept a cocktail of defeats in the twilight of his presidency (from an escalating and unpopular war to ceding the selection of the new chief justice to a hated political adversary), so did Obama resort to executive action not requiring congressional coordination in the final years of his. Noticeably absent from such activities was staffing the federal courts, for it cannot be done unilaterally.

Inaugurated into a glut of judicial vacancies, Obama then passed to his successor a stockpile of appointment opportunities, as his final months in office succumbed to a particularly punctilious application of the Thurmond Rule. One president's handicap is another's windfall. This brings us to the final factor in the mix of political conditions that inform a president's judicial appointment strategy: judicial vacancies, their number, and their type. How do these affect when Senate actors will be motivated and mobilized to succeed in opposing a president's judicial selections? Can or how can presidents present their candidates for such vacancies in such a way as to increase the senatorial costs—political and/or institutional—of opposing them?

A large number of judicial vacancies are clearly a boon to a new president, and it can work to his or her advantage in one way, very directly: judicial vacancies can be *so* numerous as to constitute a judicial emergency *necessitating* coordinate branch response. Case backlogs and "justice delayed, justice denied" can be spun (by a smart White House Communications Director) back onto a recalcitrant Senate to the potential electoral detriment of its members. Still, a president bestowed with the opportunity to select a great proportion of the federal judiciary—at any point in his or her tenure in office—will necessarily engender scrutiny in doing so. The suspicion, of course, will be of executive packing of the federal courts. Large numbers of vacant judgeships, especially large numbers of vacancies concentrated in a single or several federal circuits, will thus tend to motivate whatever senatorial opposition exists.

Nothing, however, motivates and mobilizes an opposition to succeed like judicial vacancies with the capacity to alter the partisan balance of a particular court. This is why a depleted court circuit—a federal circuit court of appeals—fires up a president's political opponents: they know that the more of such concentrated vacancies exist, the more likely that the president can make particular circuits and panels of judges within those circuits in his or her image, by replenishing the bulk of their personnel to populate *en banc* and panel majorities. Such vacancy distribution is less of a factor for the battle over federal district court judgeships, whose judges sit alone and as triers of fact, and so have less capacity to function as a partisan-inflected unit. With federal district court vacancies, it is the total or overall number that figures in the appointment process context, less so whether and where they are geographically clustered.[2]

The partisan-balance altering variable applies most pointedly to vacant seats on the Supreme Court, in one of two ways. First, the court may be fragmented and polarized into opposing voting blocs, where the majority-making balance of power lies with the vote of a centrist justice. A president may then be called upon to replace this court center, likely a moderate, who may have been appointed by a previous president from either party. Altering the court's composition by filling a "swing" justice's seat has great potential to immediately shift the court's political majority to the left or the right, so such appointments are among the most significant a president can make. Unfortunately, because of this, they are also those that Senate actors will be most motivated and mobilized to succeed in opposing. (Bork was such a candidate, nominated to replace the court centrist and moderate Republican Lewis Powell.) Added to that is the fact that replacing a swing vote with one that is less so helpfully supplies the Senate opposition with a rhetorical plan of attack. Since by definition almost any (liberal or conservative) candidate a (liberal or conservative) president could name would be more ideologically left or right than a moderate centrist, Senate opponents can easily and plausibly position themselves as against a president's placing of ideological extremists on the bench. Most of the time, then, in this swing seat appointment scenario, a president will be under duress to present his or her nominee as a restrained and technically motivated jurist, possessing gravitas and judicial temperament, if not palpably moderate in his or her inclinations. Such packaging will be necessary to diffuse and deflect opposition efforts at stalling, blocking, and defeating a president's ideologically preferred substitute for the departing swing justice. Greater presidential compromise, to the point of selecting and putting forth a truly centrist, nonpartisan, and agenda-less candidate, would be required only in the case of a hostile and powerful Senate majority.

The second Supreme Court scenario that presents a vacancy with partisan balance of power implications is the retirement or departure of a justice whose voting record is directly at odds with the president's own legal policy vision. When that justice has also been critical to if not the leader of a judicial voting bloc, his or her replacement can change a reliable court majority into a frustrated dissenting faction. A conservative Republican president replacing a liberal lion on a court generally dominated by a liberal majority can seriously diminish if not effectively dismantle that legal liberalism; the converse is of course true for a liberal, Democratic president. Often, this occurs because the president's appointee—being, say, a conservative-voting in place of a liberal-voting justice—has shifted the court's median point to the right of where it had been. This changes the identity of the median justice, who now may be a person much more right-of-center than the previous median, and thus much more likely to complete or augment right-leaning voting majorities. The previous median justice, while still on the court and presumably still voting the same ways, is no longer so pivotal and is more marginalized within a minority bloc.

While dramaturgical senatorial opposition is energized by such right-to-left or left-to-right court nominations, no senator really expects a president to proffer his or her ideological opposite. Presidents have to replace justices appointed by presidents of the opposing party, elections have consequences, and the president's prerogative is to make policy-oriented judicial appointments. When liberal court icons William Brennan and Thurgood Marshall retired due to deteriorating health, yielding their seats to Republican President George H. W. Bush, it was understood that he would fill them with more conservative jurists. In David Souter, his replacement for Brennan, Bush and his aides clearly hoped that the former's "stealth" status—his lack of a definitive paper trail as to his legal and political preferences and commitments—would raise senators' informational costs in building a case to credibly derail him. Souter, of course, would reveal himself on the court to be much more progressively inclined than anyone expected—and despite the pledges of assurance as to his conservative bona fides from former Republican governor and Bush Chief of Staff John Sununu. Bush found a more certain and durable conservative in Clarence Thomas, who succeeded Marshall as only the second African-American on the High Court; Thomas' confirmation, however, was beset with challenges to his qualifications other than ideology—to put it mildly. Thomas' tremendous difficulties as a candidate had less to do with the fact that he was a black conservative proposed as replacement for a black liberal (although some, Thomas included, would contest this proposition) and more to do with his slim professional credentials and questionable professional behaviors. His ultimately but albeit narrowly successful confirmation vote was a Senate concession to the reality of the situation: that as long as the Republican president obeyed the demographic (in this case, racial) appointment imperative, he was entitled to a justice reflecting his own party's legal agenda.

The nomination and confirmation of Thomas began a slow and steady creep to the right on the Supreme Court, as recent Republican presidents have mostly selected justices appreciably more conservative than their predecessors while recent Democratic presidents mostly replaced moderates with other moderate—or, occasionally, a left-of-center anomaly like Ford-era Republican John Paul Stevens with a true liberal, in this instance Obama's Elena Kagan. The upshot of this trend is that the inevitably upcoming Supreme Court vacancies present the GOP with much to gain and the Democrats with much to potentially lose. At this writing, the Kennedy swing seat remains the plum for either party, but a fruit very much out of reach for lame-duck President Barack Obama. Elderly justices cluster at either end of the court's left–right continuum, but Obama's waning time in office and opposition-party-dominated Senate make his replacing any Republican-appointed jurist a proposition of zero probability. Even the filling of one of the two Clinton-appointee seats—a selection that would simply keep pace with the current left–right alignment on the bench—is rather unlikely. Vacancy hoarding by the Senate Republicans has already begun and is effectuated by a variety of Senate veto procedures, the topic to which we now turn.

The Institutional Setting and the Array of Senatorial Veto Points as Constraints

Retaining or reserving judicial vacancies for an incoming president who is hopefully going to be a fellow partisan is a senator's job. And it necessitates utilizing senatorial obstruction tactics against a current chief executive's judicial staffing efforts. The previous section delineated the political conditions in place that will or will not increase the likelihood of Senate opposition to presidential judicial selections; this section catalogs the procedural tools of that opposition and assesses the ways presidents can surmount them.

The procedural tools of Senate obstruction are the stuff of parliamentary tactical strategy. The tools are Senate rules, formal and informal, that delineate how and when senatorial vetoes may be deployed. The value of vetoes is that they constrain presidential freedom of action, appointment-wise. Some veto points are temporary, meaning they are devices to delay or stall nominations; others are points of closure that terminate a nomination. Of the latter, the most obvious is a floor vote not to confirm a nominee, which defeats by a simple majority the candidate's prospects for joining the federal judiciary, at least for that time being. Failed nominees are seldom if ever resubmitted for consideration. They are a tremendous loss for a president,[3] but they also exact a tremendous cost from Senate majorities in terms of time, resources, political energies, and potentially punishing political exposure for a senator's own floor vote yes or no. Other, more covert versions of senatorial vetoes are thus attractive options, most of which have the added benefit of essentially killing a nomination while maintaining the fiction of continuing to study it.

The Majority Leader, the Senate Judiciary Committee, its chair, its individual members, and individual senators all have veto maneuvers at their disposal. Unlike the floor vote to defeat a confirmation, these vetoes are better described as impediments or obstacles to confirmation. Although their exercise can in practice be fatal to a nomination, they do not procedurally terminate it. A partial exception is the case of the blue slip practice, which permits a home state senator to communicate his or her objection to a presidential nominee, normally a federal district or circuit court candidate. This objection is sought by and communicated to the Senate Judiciary Committee, early in the confirmation trajectory. The use of the blue slip likely began to reduce uncertainty about the prospects of the president's nominees on the Senate floor; the term originates in the color of the paper used for the sheets issued. A negative blue slip was originally intended to be advisory, leaving in the Judiciary Committee chair's hands the decision as to how to proceed, given this early warning of a home state senator's lack of assent. It was seldom given the status of an absolute veto; instead, the chair would typically choose to proceed with reservations and seek additional information on the nominee. But the result intended or otherwise would be to stall the progress of the judicial candidacy. Automatically tabling a "blue-slipped" nomination was the announced practice of very few committee chairs, and the exploitation of the blue slip practice by a president's partisan foes is a fairly recent development. Still, the blue slip veto point can be a fatal one, as it was during the committee chairmanship of conservative Southern Democrat Senator James Eastland, from 1956 to 1978. GOP conservative Orrin Hatch, on the other hand, abolished the blue slip system entirely during the second Bush administration, having reinstated the practice—which had lapsed—during Clinton's Democratic administration, when Hatch also served as Judiciary Committee Chair. Subsequent chairs have tempered such extremes but the practice has been fully restored and been taken full advantage of by individual senators, who can also attempt to delay action on nominations by simply declining to return a completed blue slip to the committee. As a stratagem, this is a temporary obstruction, but it is a potentially irritating one just the same.

With respect to obstruction that keeps a nomination in procedural limbo, such senatorial vetoing constrains the president by forcing him or her to expend additional time on an appointment and perhaps devote additional energy with efforts to remove the block. It is a costliness strategy, in other words. Senators use obstruction to attempt to wait a president out, for extended time is no nominee's friend. With time comes more opportunity for damning information to surface, just as elapsed time puts a nominee's own life and career plans on hold. For most nominees, there is a point at which too long is too long and they withdraw their name from consideration. This must be considered a victory for the president's Senate opponents, and a senatorial veto as a successful choke point.

All obstructionist maneuvers depend for their effectiveness on some degree of institutional complicity from the Senate leadership. This is obviously the case for those maneuvers that involve committee decisions *not* to schedule confirmation hearings and *not* to hold or to report committee votes on judicial nominees to the floor—decisions that lie with the committee chair who is, by virtue of the Senate's own organizing rules, part of the party leadership. Both such committee actions are stalls: one of the advice-giving dimension and senatorial scrutiny of the president's nominee and the other of the consent-giving aspect of senatorial rendering of an opinion on confirmation. Both stalls are also acts of omission and, as such, are veto points exercised by a chair of the Judiciary Committee who is presumably empowered by a supportive committee majority. Committee members may themselves be the perpetrators of committee-based obstruction maneuvers, using their power of withholding assent to move forward with committee procedures. Again, that committee majority may be substantially less friendly and thus more obstructionist of the president than the Senate majority as a whole. Indeed, the committee may report a negative majority vote to the floor, indicating that the committee does not recommend confirmation. The committee may also report a majority vote of "no recommendation"—a damning with faint praise if there ever was, which a 13–1 majority of the committee did in 1991 with respect to the nomination of Clarence Thomas for the Supreme Court.

With all this in mind, presidents must remember that stalls or even negative committee votes do not kill a nomination, but they belabor its progress through the Senate's advice and consent procedures—at times to the point of frustration and surrender on the part of a nominee. If a president is to forestall this conclusion to events, his or her intervention will require mobilizing Senate leaders or otherwise influential Senate allies from outside the committee to put pressure on and/or make trade-offs with the committee chair to move things along. In the case of the imperiled Thomas nomination, Bush aides and interest group allies waged a media campaign on the candidate's behalf, particularly in the South where the Republican Party had built a base. This threat of GOP encroachment indirectly pressured Southern Democratic senators to vote yes, for fear a no vote would cost them future electoral support with African-American voters—a segment of their electorates critical to their reelection. (This, in spite of Thomas' obvious departures—as a black conservative—from the viewpoint of the civil rights community.) For the scenario of presidential persuasion to promise success, a president often needs to draw on his or her own political capital, such as public popularity, electoral leverage, or influence with key party coalition members, interest group, and otherwise. Appealing to each type of capital can constitute an overture that can overcome a procedural barrier or sway a senator's vote on confirmation.

Committee bottlenecks and nay-saying are at least public, known, out in the open. Even negative and tardy blue slips on particular judicial candidates are now matters reported for the public record, as are the blue slip protocols of presiding chairs of the Judiciary Committee. Fingers can be pointed, blame can be leveled. Presidents can rail against specific senators and Senate leaders. But some Senate veto points are cloaked in anonymity and are the provenance of any one of the amorphous mass of senators in the body as a whole. Of course, these too depend for their obstructive force on the acquiescence of the Senate leadership as the standard-bearers of the institution's practices. Of these more hidden-from-view sorts of vetoes, the most important is the hold—important because it is a meaningful blockage that *is* accepted as practice. Informally formal like the blue slip procedure, the hold depends for its parameters and effectiveness on the assent of the Senate majority and its Majority Leader. Also like the blue slip procedure, the credible threat of a filibuster is the source of the power of the covert veto operation that is the hold.

The hold originated as a legislative colleague's courtesy request for additional time to study a legislative matter, for delay in proceeding to allow for the gathering of more information before casting a vote, including on a nominated judicial candidate. Although holds can be publicly disclosed and wholly legitimate exercises, more common is the hold that is communicated privately, to the senator's party leadership. These too ostensibly have an expiration date at which time the senator in question must announce him or herself and the reason for the hold request. Such expiration dates, and the reciprocal courtesy extended for them, have been extending over recent decades, and the period for which a hold is in place can also be expanded through what judicial scholar Amy Steigerwalt calls "revolving holds": tag-team holds, whereby an allied group of senators each follows a colleague's expiring anonymous hold on a nomination with a fresh one (Steigerwalt 2010, 76). In practice, then, the hold is a tactic for stalling that requires no real justification, has few negative repercussions attached to its exercise, and exerts a vise grip on a judicial candidate's future as an appointee. This is because holds discourage the majority leader from asking for unanimous consent to call up nominations in the Senate's executive session, as holds are implicitly withholding consent to move forward. Holds signal opposition. The implicit threat—the consequence of defying it—is a filibuster that can preclude that unanimous consent and, thus, an up-or-down vote to confirm a nominee.

The hold illustrates that the majority leader has tremendous power to expedite, or not to expedite, blocked or otherwise impeded judicial nominations. The majority leader ultimately determines whether to go into executive session for the full Senate's consideration of the nomination—for the confirmation vote, in other words. And—significantly—the majority leader may alter procedural rules, and in so doing avert the deployment of the filibuster, by an ordinary majoritarian vote. This is what occurred under Majority Leader Harry Reid in November 2013. Frustrated by the obstructionism of the Senate Republican minority with respect to Obama's lower federal court appointments, Reid exercised his option as leader to eliminate the 60-vote requirement to end a filibuster. Triggered by GOP senators' stalemating of Obama candidates for three vacancies for the powerful and pivotal Court of Appeals for the District of Columbia Circuit, the rules change was effected by a majority vote, of which the Democrats were in control, and applied only to filibusters of presidential nominees for lower federal courts and the executive branch.

Reid put into practice what the prior Republican Majority Leader Bill Frist had threatened to do when the then-Democratic minority was filibustering several of George W. Bush's most controversial contenders for court of appeals slots. At that time labeled the "nuclear option," the rules change was evaded when a bipartisan "Gang of Fourteen" senators agreed to a compromise in May 2005, allowing five of the ten filibustered nominees to be confirmed. The compromise included the agreement that "neither party would filibuster block judicial nominees except in 'extraordinary circumstances,' with an apparent understanding that ideology would not be considered 'extraordinary'" (Schwartz 2014). This informal agreement did not last, and ideological objections from opposition-party senators to Obama's selections began in 2009 when he took office—thus (eventually) engendering the Reid power play. Reid's action greatly benefited President Obama's staffing of the federal courts; Reid's action also illustrates rather dramatically how partisan and vacancy variables interact with veto point procedures. His ability to marshal a majority to circumvent minority obstruction via filibustering was completely a product of presidential same-party control of the Senate. His impetus to do so, moreover, was directly a product of Republican resistance to partisan balance shifts on the D.C. Circuit Court: the vacancies Obama was attempting to fill would allow Democratic appointees to assume a majority of the active judges for the circuit's panels. Extraordinary action by the majority leader was necessary to overcome the minority's strong incentive to deploy whatever vetoes were at its disposal.

Of course, what one majority leader can do another can undo. As the alternating policies of Judiciary Committee chairs on the blue slip custom illustrate, Senate leaders can be effective presidential allies or effective presidential opponents. Only the latter operate as true constraints on a president's appointment practices, but a same-party leader who is a vacillating weakling can be almost as bad. Because so many Senate veto points depend on a majority leader and a Judiciary Committee chair who are willing to tolerate them, presidents in some way have the easy part of supplying the names for staffing the federal courts—with the president's Senate doing the hard work of turning those names into judges. Even a same-party Senate must labor to do so, and fashioning and refashioning Senate procedural rules can definitely be part of that labor. Yet it and its ensuing results are, maddeningly, mostly outside a president's ambit of control.

At times, extra-institutional, extra-senatorial actors and factors must be brought to bear on deadlocked or negatively trending Senates, as George H. W. Bush did with his party's evangelical interest group allies in the Thomas situation. Unfortunately for presidents, interest groups can also serve other masters, as well as pursue independent courses of their own in the judicial appointment process.

The Interest Group Dimension

There is thus one final element in the presidential calculus of the institutional setting and political context of his or her appointments to the federal judiciary. As such, it is also an element of profound importance to senators in their collective effort to assert advice and consent authority. Senators, too, make strategic calculations about when the time is ripe for exercising particular procedural vetoes against a president's putative appointees. But how do senators inform themselves as to relevant political conditions and, more significantly, qualities specific to the judicial candidates themselves that make them more or less vulnerable to opposition and attack? Conversely, how do presidents determine how their nominees are being received by the public and whether to battle for their passage through the various pitfalls of Senate confirmation? The answer is interest groups.

Interest group participation impacts both senatorial and Judiciary Committee behavior and public opinion responses to the president's prospective judges. Interest groups have been at the center of more than one of the mileposts in the exercise of judicial appointment power discussed in Chapter 1. Their involvement, particularly their activism in successfully opposing Supreme Court nominee Robert Bork, was a transformational moment for the appointment process. Post-Bork, interest group activity has expanded to the lower federal court confirmation context, as these judgeships have morphed from patronage-based to policy-based appointments. Interest groups' informational, signaling, and packaging behaviors are critical elements of the nominee's journey in and a president's successful navigation through the politico-institutional setting of the appointment process. If confirmation of nominees is about presciently reading the tea leaves of partisanship, presidential political capital, and senatorial vetoing, interest groups can help a president to do so. They can also magnify the force of any one of the political and institutional impediments that a president encounters, and thus greatly hinder or completely handicap his or her judicial staffing efforts.

The interest group dimension spans the nomination, the pre-confirmation hearings, the hearings public event, and the committee and full Senate confirmation voting stages of judicial appointment. Their informational function is most important during the earliest stages of the process and is just as it sounds: collecting and analyzing information on nominees, their background, policy views, and any controversial decisions they have made. Interest groups can be formal or more informal sources of information. The American Bar Association, discussed in Chapter 1, has been since the early 1950s a part of the formal stream of information generated on each nominee for the federal bench. Different presidents have paid different degrees of heed to this information and its source, with the ABA's professional ratings being disregarded by the second Bush administration in favor of evaluations from more conservative-networked legal interest groups. But the important point about the ABA is that it is a private (non-governmental) association that is formally integrated into the nomination and confirmation process in an advisory capacity. Moreover, the professional information it gathers and the estimation it renders are available to all the governmental parties in the process: the president's office and the members of the Senate. Yet judicial nominations strain the resources of the Senate, and it is here that interest groups as an informal source of information play a role. Interest groups' assembling and reviewing of information on nominees helps senators sort through the voluminous amounts of information provided through formal sources, such as the nominees' own questionnaires and filed documents, FBI background checks, and the ABA's reports. With limited staff and lack of time, members of the Senate and particularly of the Judiciary Committee depend on interest groups to differentiate among the many pending nominations and to identify which nominees require additional attention. Interest groups used to fulfill this role by testifying at confirmation hearings; with this formal participation now curtailed, interest groups use informal transmission avenues such as written communiqués to committee and senatorial staffers and lobbying efforts.

While the president and committee senators focus on the nominees' background and views, the vast majority of senators care about constituency considerations and home state political calculations with respect to judicial candidates. Interest groups and their local affiliates become the conduits for such home style-tailored information. Conversely, national-level interest group organizations that are presidential allies or partisan coalition partners become useful conduits of their own, but for media and public relations coordinated with the White House. In other words, information about judicial nominees flowing from interest groups to the Senate may either compete with or complement information managed by the president's office.

The signaling function in interest groups' behavior in the appointment process is even more critical to senatorial response to judicial nominees and, so, even more important for a president to monitor. As Amy Steigerwalt summarizes it, in her 2010 study *Battle Over the Bench*:

> "Groups must decide whether they will publicly object to the nominee and wage a campaign to defeat him or her. Because of limited resources, groups cannot oppose every nominee, and so they strategically and sparingly oppose objectionable nominees. These objections raise a 'fire alarm' and send valuable ideological and institutional clues to senators about the nomination." (p. 118)

Judicial watchdog groups of the left and the right specialize in "fire alarming" and thus filling a critically important information gap for senators: identifying those nominees who are worth blocking and/or defeating. Such interest group signaling action has powerful consequences for the tone of the nomination, veto deployment, and the number of negative votes it will likely receive at the confirmation stage, if not its ultimate outcome. Senators listen to such alarms because they risk political retaliation—the interest group's mobilization of home state electoral opposition—if they do not. Among the factors, then, that a senator must evaluate is whether the signaling group is one whose organizational good opinion (and campaign donation monies) matter for his or her standing with key segments of the state electorate.

Interest groups also raise alarms to remind presidents that extreme or otherwise objectionable nominee choices will entail executive diversion of resources away from other legislative priorities in order to campaign for embattled judicial candidates. While senators can and do discount and even ignore interest group signaling, presidents should not. Presidents must know that nominations moved into the public limelight because of negative media attention *fomented by* interest group press releases are nominations delayed. Receptive, vulnerable, and key senators are cued into a more cautious mode of analysis and a more studied reception of the nominee and the political consequences of supporting or not supporting him or her. If this time of caution and reflection is to work in favor of and not against the president and his or her nominee, it must be filled with information that counteracts or at least neutralizes the negative and the critical. This, too, of course must be filtered and assessed by various senators—obliging further stalling—but if the counter-story is absent, interest group fire alarms will trigger a cascade of Senate opposition to the nominee.

Following, therefore, closely on the heels of interest groups' signaling behavior is their packaging function in the judicial appointment process. The point at which nominees confront public objections to their nominations by interest groups is the point at which the confirmation becomes both a partisan and a public relations exercise. This unleashes the "war of the airwaves" or the dueling narratives stage of the appointment saga. Interest groups are to be found on both sides of the contest to package the nominee and the nomination in general. Interest groups also have a multitude of motives for being actively involved in the judicial appointment process and for weighing in on a specific nomination in particular: organizational maintenance, alliance building, symbolic politics, as well as actual instrumental outcomes: securing or defeating a particular nominee or nominees. As a matter of institutional dynamics, interest group attack campaigns provide political cover and/or justification for senators to veto or otherwise vote in the negative on a judicial candidate. More substantively, packaging occurs during the later stages of the appointment process—in the lead-up to the confirmation hearings, during them, and immediately after—and for interest groups at this point, the goal is to supplant a positive frame of reference for the nominee with a negative or uncomplimentary one. Often, what is at stake is which side—pro- or anti-nominee—can activate in the public's mind a preexisting frame of reference favorable to the nominee. For the president and his or her interest group allies and surrogates, this means presenting judicial candidates—if not preemptively framing them—in terms of legalistic criteria like judiciousness and professional merit. Such criteria tap into a reservoir of good feeling and respect for the legitimacy of the judiciary. For fire alarming and other oppositional interest groups, the task of packaging is to trigger the popular antipathy to judicial "activism" and substitute a frame of ideology, partisanship, and policy making that undermines that very legitimacy of the candidate as a potential jurist.

Interest group packaging is indeed directed at the public, at ordinary people, because the mobilization of constituents (i.e., people) is a natural pressure point on senators. Furthermore, nominations subject to dueling packaging/dueling narratives—as was Samuel Alito's to the US Supreme Court—succeed "in considerable part owing to the failure of interest groups to mobilize public opinion against the nomination" (Gibson and Caldeira 2009, 126). Using Alito's long years of experience as a federal appellate judge and his amassed record of deliberate if conservative judicial decisions, his proponents in the Bush White House convincingly framed him in terms of legal professionalism, while the liberal group affiliates critical of his record were unable to gain traction with their depiction of Alito as an ideologue and a GOP political hack. Put more tactically, a president's interest group allies and surrogates must package the nominee in such a way as to increase the potential senatorial costs—political and/or institutional—of opposing him or her. This includes offensive and defensive framing of the nominee in a light that induces public support, as well as framing a batch of nominees (for lower federal court vacancies, obviously) *as a batch* that highlights the positive qualities that apply to all of them—usually, legalistic qualities that evoke underlying public support for the judicial institution. If such positive frames stick in the public mind—due to successful pro-nominee packaging—wavering senators have a much harder time justifying their oppositional stance and are disinclined to be brave enough to so act, lest they pay for it later at the polls.

Quite obviously, presidents engage in a good deal of packaging of their nominees—preemptively and otherwise—and presidents and their staff direct a good bit of the offensive and defensive framing of and choice of frames for said nominees. But presidents can also lose the upper hand or otherwise lose control of the framing exercise to packaging efforts by oppositional interest groups, as happened during the Bork confirmation experience. At times, this loss is a presidential cost–benefit concession; at other times, it is a miscalculation or outright blunder. Interest groups make the advice and consent terrain that much more treacherous to navigate when they work in concert with a president's party opponents and give aid and comfort to those (senators) with institutional powers to object to presidential staffing choices.

Confirmation is a more publically accountable and democratic process as a result of interest group involvement, but this feature also narrows and constrains presidential options in that "regardless of the nature of the nominee a president is almost certain to face organized opposition" (Silverstein 2007, 228). What a president must calculate—what interest groups and their informational, signaling, and packaging activities assist the president in calculating—are the advantages and disadvantages of any appointment opportunity and the extent to which a judicial vacancy is more of a "no win" political liability than a "no lose" policy asset. A suitable candidate does not always exist for the former, but the assortment of confirmable candidates for the latter is considerable; the strategic presidential actor does not confuse the two situations and understands the range that exists in between them.

The Context of Judicial Appointment: A Coda

Minimizing uncertainty is about appreciating the politico-institutional factors that condition reception and reaction, by senators, interest groups, and the general public, with respect to a president's judicial appointees. Appointment is interdependent choice, in the strategic sense; the astute president appreciates which factors must be accepted as constraints and which can be played to his or her advantage. The next chapter integrates the lessons of the previous two and offers a "how to" manual for the modern chief executive who is staffing the courts in the bright light of public scrutiny, senatorial skepticism, and competing claims from his own coalition.

Notes

1. As well as general disinterest, for until the 1970s there were few policy consequences attached to the appointment of lower federal court judges. Senators routinely deferred to presidential prerogative as well as to the preferences of home-state senators, for whom a lower court nominee was a patronage/state party politics matter.
2. Except in the situation where a category of contentious federal cases are regionally concentrated, as were the school desegregation orders managed by Southern federal district judges during the 1960s and early 1970s following the *Brown v. Board of Education* decision.
3. Presidents can nevertheless use troubled and failed nominees to rally their partisan supporters, in a strategic effort known as "going public" with a nominee. Of course, it is still an effort to recoup something beneficial from what is undeniably a setback.

FOUR

How

If there is a central lesson to the previous chapter, it is that a president can neither be afraid of nor paralyzed by political uncertainty as he or she assesses the political and institutional appointment context through which nominees must travel to become federal judges. Rather, a president must identify and understand the contextual elements and factors that allow him or her to reduce that uncertainty.

Clearly, uncertainty also bedevils the presidential assessment of his or her prospective nominees. Chapter 2 attempted to detail what correlations are known between various candidate qualities and qualifications and their performance as judges. But it is also their performance as nominees in the confirmation hearing before the Senate Judiciary Committee that a nominating president would hope to predict and, if possible, orchestrate to a successful conclusion.

There is a recipe of ingredients and steps for the president to follow in successfully "packing" the courts. The attentive reader of the previous chapters of this presidential briefing book will suspect that that recipe contains both candidate- and context-related elements as well as lessons from the history of federal judicial appointment. Not surprisingly, the two core components in staffing the federal judiciary are candidate *screening* and executive *staffing*. All else is secondary, or a subsidiary of one of these two components.

Informed by historical developments but oriented toward the contemporary presidential era, this fourth chapter takes as its point of departure the watershed and model that is the Reagan

Administration, whose success in shaping the contours and thus the output of the federal courts was essentially a matter of smart personnel decisions. Such decisions are made at two levels: identifying and sponsoring the right judicial candidates, and creating and building a coterie of White House and Justice Department staff dedicated to the project. At both levels—securing the best judicial appointees and naming key judicial appointment staffers—a president is counseled to take advantage of ideological networks or, where these are undeveloped or nonexistent, to establish and nurture them.

The chapter opens with a brief mention of President Jimmy Carter's merit selection and judicial diversity commissions for federal circuit court appointments and reveals that despite coming to the Senate with a strong presumption of competence, his nominees to the lower federal courts were among the first to face the "modern" era of politicized scrutiny. Carter's effort to centralize and organize judicial staffing to accomplish executive partisan and policy goals was the inspiration for later and more fulsome presidential exercises in judicial and judicial selection personnel management. The chapter then reiterates some of the most important accomplishments of Ronald Reagan in this area and reviews the template he put in place. Comparison of the performance of the most recent presidents George W. Bush and Barack Obama will then be conducted, with relevant lessons learned from their accomplishments (or lack thereof) extrapolated.

This chapter delineates the "how" to effectively staff the courts, with recommendations for adapting the twin, core components of candidate screening and executive staffing to the president's own individual circumstances.

Candidate Screening and Executive Staffing: Intertwined in the Reagan Template

It would be an exaggeration to claim that the Reagan Administration invented the screening of judicial candidates and the naming of a presidential staff dedicated to judicial selection. Precursors obviously exist, but as Chapter 1 on "History" explained, the president's Article II appointment power developed its modern, expansive utilization only gradually. And the senatorial role in nomination and confirmation was prominent, and significant. Yet while staffing of the lower federal courts was, until relatively recently, "senatorial appointment with the advice and consent of the Senate,"[1] explicitly presidential efforts to identify suitable if not ideal Supreme Court nominees nevertheless have a long history.

In the presidency's early, pre-administrative management days, those efforts lacked programmatic direction. The judicial appointment process was also relatively closed up through the Civil War period, with participation limited to the president and senators. Presidents relied on party colleagues and to some degree the partisan press for feedback on potential nominees. But only Senate partisans could be considered "part" of the president's own screening of judicial candidates, and even the information and assistance provided by the attorney general of a president's Justice Department played a limited and subordinate role. Cabinet members and organized interests, in business and labor, attempted to lobby presidents, from the 1880s onward, yet their consultation remained an informal rather than a formally integrated part of a screening process. This situation all changed with the 1939 passage of the Reorganization Act, through which the president gained major staff resources in the creation of the Executive Office of the President and the White House Office. These assets of the "institutional presidency" made possible an active presidential role in domestic policy formation, including policy leadership on judicial staffing. WHO in particular was designed to contain personal, political staff responsive to the sitting president, who would change from one administration to the next—indeed, all of the units designed (by the various presidents who saw them created) to help the president in the judicial and especially Supreme Court selection process are part of the White House Office personnel: the Office of Communications, the Congressional Liaison Office, the Office of Public Liaison, and the Office of the White House Counsel. As the titles of these various offices indicate, their presence made possible the presidential orchestration of input from and influence on senatorial and interest group actors. While Richard Nixon was the first president to take full advantage of all these institutional assets, their operations under him were still diffuse and relatively uncoordinated.

Reagan's most important immediate precedent in the design of the screening and staffing for judicial selection was Jimmy Carter and his conscious campaign to remake the lower federal courts. By executive order and just one month from taking office in 1977, Carter created the US Circuit Judge Nominating Commission, charged with nominating judges for the federal courts of appeals based on merit and diversity considerations. Carter's Justice Department developed detailed guidelines for the operation of the nominating commissions in each circuit. Composed of lawyers and nonlawyers and ostensibly balanced in terms of partisanship, Carter's White House-appointed commissions recommended from three to five well-qualified persons to the president for his consideration; most observers agree that Carter's approach substantially increased the racial and gender diversity of the federal bench. Of course, he was helped in this endeavor by two things: first, the successful reorganization of the existing Fifth Circuit Court of Appeals and the creation of the new Eleventh Circuit in 1980, which presented the opportunity to fill a new court's worth of federal appellate judgeships and, second, by the dramatic expansion in the total size of the federal bench (circuit and district levels) in the Omnibus Judgeship Act of 1978. Both new vacancies windfalls fell to him.

But these staffing accomplishments came at a cost: with his nominating commissions undermining traditional senatorial courtesy in the advice portion of the advice and consent process, Carter angered his partisan opponents in the Senate who suspected more base political motives behind his ostensibly meritorious appointments initiative. Clearly, diversifying the federal bench in terms of racial minority and women appointees played to key interests within the Democratic Party coalition and had an obvious electoral angle. Carter's nominating commissions initiative was surely part of his larger political agenda of inclusiveness for "outsider" groups, but he presented his idea for judicial staffing as deemphasizing partisanship and ideology as considerations. Whether he was sincere or not or whether he was simply playing politics with judicial selection under the guise of its impersonal bureaucratization is not the point: what is was Carter's centralization of judicial nomination within executive operations, altering the institutional dynamic of the judicial appointment power in the president's favor.

This fact remains, even though his successor Ronald Reagan abolished Carter's nominating commission structure. In leaving his own indelible mark on the staffing of the federal judiciary, Reagan built upon the premise of centralization, adding systematic screening of candidates and ideological loyalty of staffers doing it into the mix. Neither nonpartisan merit selection nor ethnic and gender diversity for diversity's sake was of much interest to the Reagan White House. Rather, a formalized machinery for policy-oriented judicial appointments was. It is no exaggeration to say that, at both the levels of intention and execution, Reagan influenced the selection and the composition of the federal judiciary like no president before him.

This began with the creation in 1981 of the President's Committee on Federal Judicial Selection as part of WHO, concentrating power within and further institutionalizing the role of the White House in selecting federal judges. Reagan also restructured the Justice Department, giving its Office of Legal Policy broad but targeted responsibility for judicial selection and staff resources designed solely for the screening of judicial candidates. The corresponding, systematic screening procedures included carefully scrutinizing candidates' record of previous judicial decisions, articles, and speeches for their philosophical orientation and bringing leading candidates for judicial positions to Washington for extensive interviewing by OLP staff. Coordinated by Reagan's Attorney General Edwin Meese, the point of such background investigation was to certify that a prospective nominee "reasoned from constitutional premises" and adhered to " jurisprudence of original intent" with the goal to use judicial appointment "to institutionalize the Reagan revolution so it can't be set aside no matter what happens in future presidential elections" (Quoted passages from Maltese 1995, 122–3).

Despite this seemingly straightforward policy-oriented focus, complicated overlapping responsibilities between White House staff—such as the chief of staff and the White House Counsel—and Justice Department operatives occasionally produced internal power struggles over the best judicial nominees and the strategies for their confirmation. A telling example was the failed Bork nomination. The Reagan team did not always see eye-to-eye, but dissonance within a large, complex staff organization is to be expected from time to time in the nature of things. A president must manage and stand ready to adjudicate such disagreements; there must be a clear chain of command that ultimately prevails. In Reagan's case that chain led upwards to Attorney General Meese, who was the president's close friend if not alter ego on matters of constitutional politics. The Reagan Justice Department's social policy agenda was largely framed in opposition to Warren and Burger Court rulings on school prayer, abortion, and affirmative action; this priority carried and carried into the judicial selection machinery of OLP *and* WHO. In this there was no confusion.

One important factor aided in disciplining attention to this priority: the existence of and reliance on a key ideological network. The Reagan Administration was the first to take advantage of the support structure provided by a "shadow" ABA: the conservative, academically oriented network of the Federalist Society, which began its operation as a "safe harbor" for conservative legal intellectuals, law students, and, later, judges and public interest law groups in 1982. The Federalist Society sought to provide a counterbalance to the liberal jurisprudence that prevailed in law schools at that time, by developing an alternative, historically textual method of constitutional interpretation and a similarly revised understanding of the proper role of the federal judge in American democracy. The society largely achieves its goal of influencing law and legal policy by educating Republican and other conservatively oriented lawyers. This is because from early on, Federalist Society patronage became a pipeline for employment opportunities as administration counsel, law clerk, and federal judge. With affiliation came sponsorship, connections to the conservative elite—both within and outside the Reagan White House.

Although the Federalist Society, as a loose association of membership chapters, eschewed official dogma or the taking of policy positions, its principles were clearly concordant with the Reagan Republicans. As one former assistant attorney general during Reagan's second term characterized the interconnection: "The Federalist Society helped to identify, to track, people who proved to be capable of filling [judicial] positions . . .[and] also helped to create more individuals who found [conservative legal] views attractive" (Quoted in Teles 2008, 158). That Meese himself would "retire" to Federalist Society "experts" status (and a simultaneous leadership post with the conservative Washington think tank the Heritage Foundation) after leaving the Reagan Justice Department speaks directly to the society's function in generating a personnel pool for prospective judges as well as for judicial selection staff. Indeed, the latter could graduate into the former with some ease, with the cross-fertilization between administration legal staff and judicial nominees facilitated by Federalist Society commonalities. Stamp of approval or secret handshake, Federalist Society membership verified beliefs and commitment, assuring both.

Beginning with the Reagan years, then, the Federalist Society served as a key link for the constituencies in the conservative alliance, forging connections between members that lead to new job prospects and joint projects, policy oriented and otherwise. As a network, it has played an important role in "vetting federal judicial nominees, staffing conservative public interest law groups and Republican administrations, and matching conservative [law] students with prominent conservative judges" (Southworth 2008, 138). Relying on this network as a supply source, the Reagan template for judicial selection intertwined careful screening protocols and specified staff delegations. To get some idea of the thoroughness and intensiveness of the process, it is worth quoting at length from this recent study of the operations of the conservative legal movement:

> ". . . once candidates had been identified, the OLP (Office of Legal Policy) reviewed their written work, the comments of local bar leaders, and any recommendations by members of Congress. The OLP then determined which candidates to talk to, and invited them to the DOJ (Department of Justice) for four to five hours of interviews by different DOJ lawyers . . .The OLP followed up the personal interviews by talking with public officials, bar leaders, sitting judges, and others in the candidate's home state. It then prepared a summary of each candidate's qualifications, and the attorney general selected one candidate to recommend to the president's Federal Judicial Selection Committee. The counsel to the president chaired the committee, which also included the attorney general, the deputy attorney general, and the assistant attorney general for the OLP. Officials at the White House also did their own background checks on proposed nominees." (Avery and McLaughlin 2013, 26)

What Reagan put in place—and the contemporaneous existence of the Federalist Society helped to realize—was a highly organized, highly disciplined system for producing ideologically predictable judicial nominees. The lessons of its success, both in terms of the sheer numbers and reliably conservative voting of the Reagan judges, were not lost on subsequent chief executives. An administrative machinery of judicial selection, operating under conditions of ideological discipline facilitated by the Federalist Society network of reference and recommendation, allowed the president to efficiently and effectively use the courts as a policy arm of the party and extend the policy range of the administration. Reagan's template would be both copied and improved upon, with similar successes rewarding one Republican successor in particular.

The Reagan Template and Two Presidencies' Appointments

What began with Reagan other Republican chief executives latched onto and nourished, and Democratic successors sought to emulate within their own policy circles and ideological space. For instance, the professional/ideological pathway from administration legal staffer to federal judicial nominee, mediated by the linkage of Federalist Society affiliation, was established during the Reagan era of judicial appointments; it continued to be utilized by the heir to the Reagan revolution, Reagan's former Vice President George H. W. Bush, as a methodology for seeking and verifying the legal conservatism of prospective judicial candidates. Bush appointee and appellate judge Michael Luttig, for example, began his journey to the federal bench as law clerk to then-circuit judge Antonin Scalia and to Chief Justice Warren Burger, moving to the Office of Legal Counsel and position as assistant attorney general before being nominated to the court of appeals in 1991. And while Bush's successor Democrat Bill Clinton also aspired to appoint "politician-statesmen" to the highest court, he had something rather different in mind. Clinton sought to return to the practice of earlier Democratic presidents, such as FDR, in naming justices who had spent much of their careers in political office or public service—much of it, in FDR's case, in the president's own administration. Chief Justice Earl Warren, named to the Supreme Court as Governor of California and at the time an active party operative (ironically, a Republican, and selected by Dwight Eisenhower to remove Warren as political competition), was the kind of appointee Clinton idealized: someone who would bring real-world experience, compassion, and sensitivity to the job of judging and applying the Constitution. This is not to say that Clinton's notion of judicial appointments was any more or less policy inflected than Reagan's or Bush's, only that his approach to identifying and cultivating such political nominees was difficult to systematize. Indeed, such screening and staffing was personally idiosyncratic by its very nature. In the end, of course, Clinton dropped the prospect, after his advisers failed to convince his lead candidate, Democratic Governor Mario Cuomo, to accept a Supreme Court nomination,[2] and Clinton found other, more pressing items on his political agenda that sapped the political capital he might have expended on judicial staffing.

Republican President George W. Bush, who followed Clinton and won the contested election of 2000,[3] was more explicit than his father had been in making the connection between policy and law, in both word and deed. It was thus the second Bush administration that truly nourished and furthered what Reagan had wrought with respect to presidential judicial appointment operations. Both Bushes, however, benefitted importantly from one key fact about the Federalist Society: once established as an ideological network, it continued to function—even as a "Justice Department in exile" when the Republican Party was not in office (Scherer and Miller 2009, 367–8). George W. Bush would show that his commitment to judicial staffing, united with the structural opportunities he inherited, allowed him to more perfectly pack the courts.

Running for office against Clinton's Vice President Al Gore, Bush pledged that he would appoint judges in the mold of Antonin Scalia and Clarence Thomas. As a cue, Bush's intentions and intended practices could not have been more obvious, as these GOP-appointed justices were among the most reliable conservative votes on the bench across a range of policy issues. Both promoted through their decisions the judicial philosophy strongly associated with Edwin Meese and Federalist Society principles, known as constitutional originalism. (Indeed, Scalia was an original Federalist Society law faculty adviser.) Both were also "feeders" in the Republican judicial staffing pipeline, in that their clerks frequently moved on to Republican White House and Justice Department positions and, sometimes, judicial positions of their own. Bush thus arrived in office in 2001 with a clear plan for the federal courts, and almost immediately began putting forward slates of candidates to fill multiple vacancies on the courts of appeals. Following Reagan's model but able to draw from an even deeper and more richly developed personnel base, Bush's first slate—presented with flourish at a White House East Room ceremony—included former law clerks and administration lawyers as well as former members of Bush's own legal team during the disputed Florida election battle in December of 2000. Many bore Federalist Society recommendations. Among the group was future Chief Justice John Roberts, who would be elevated to the High Court by second term president Bush in 2005.

Bush's judicial staffing machinery replicated the candidate screening operations of the Reagan administration but accentuated the role of the White House Counsel as the chair of the president's Judicial Selection Committee. Significantly, the committee both began and concluded the candidate screening and vetting process, giving greater focus. In this, Bush ran a "tighter ship" in terms of organizational structure and ideologically disciplined decision making than even Reagan had, due to the prominent and preeminent role given to committee and counsel. Such streamlined operations made possible another strategic advance by the Bush administration: the concerted preparation of nominees for the confirmation hearing experience. Nominees had been testifying before the Senate Judiciary Committee for several decades, but television coverage of the hearings began only with Reagan-nominee Sandra Day O'Connor's appearance before the committee in 1981—the historic, first formal consideration of a woman candidate for the Supreme Court. Evidence of candidate preparation in the form of judicial selection staff guidance as to how to respond to particular senatorial questions can be seen in the O'Connor case: then-special assistant to the Attorney General John Roberts wrote then-Judge O'Connor a memo arguing against openly answering questions about specific cases or "live issues," as such candor would give the appearance of impropriety—a handy piece of advice, as it would also provide potential ammunition to O'Connor opponents in the Senate.[4] By 1993 and with Clinton-nominee Ruth Bader Ginsburg's self-imposed, blanket policy against providing previews or forecasts of how she might decide particular constitutional issues (branded the "Ginsburg Rule"), judicial nominees were schooled in a method of providing suitable but suitably vague answers to direct questions seeking legal views and opinions. Aided by (partisan) sympathetic senators lobbing "softball" questions that allowed a nominee to showcase his or her judicial image,[5] the well-prepared candidate for confirmation can thus deploy premeditated answers to generally anticipated questions. The Bush administration was particularly adept in using the preparation device of the "murder board": a mock hearing session in which White House staffers play the role of senators pressing the nominee—sessions that were "typically quite intense and may carry on for weeks at a time" (Collins and Ringhand 2013, 40).

George W. Bush also moved the once counter-establishment Federalist Society into a securely establishment role with respect to judicial selection, to where its conservative legal movement network functioned almost like an alternative governing coalition. Federalist Society members and leaders of related legal strategist organizations, like the Judicial Confirmation Network, served as official but outside, non-governmental advisers to the president on judicial selection matters and decisions. Such actors, as part of the loose affiliation of Federalist Society adherents and sympathizers, could additionally lobby publically for the president's judicial nominees, so their influence flowed both inwardly to the administration's decision making and outwardly from it, bearing its mandates. Finally, Bush also integrated his Federalist Society advisers into the established candidate evaluation process, mainly by displacing the ABA and its formal ratings of prospective judges. Announcing that the administration would not be furnishing the names of its nominees before they were submitted to the Senate or released to the public, Bush's White House Counsel Alberto Gonzales (himself a future nominee) unceremoniously communicated the ABA's removal from its historical prenomination role in the judicial appointment process. The ABA would have "no opportunity to express an opinion on a candidate for the bench until after President Bush had already made a final decision to nominate the person"—with that final decision having been influenced by a select subset of Federalist Society bar members (Avery and McLaughlin 2013, 43).

From President Bush's perspective and irrespective of what one thinks of the content of his and his judges' legal philosophy, the organizational focus of his screening and staffing process was also its ideological focus and vice versa. In this lay the strength of his judicial selection operation and the success of its results. Bush appointed a much higher proportion of Federalist Society affiliates as federal judges, and these judges were noticeably more conservative in the decisions they rendered on issues from states' rights to criminal procedure to remedying racial discrimination. By the time of Bush's tenure in office, the ideological network of the Federalist Society had also matured to the point of offering a deep reservoir of potential talent to draw from, for both staff attorneys and potential judicial nominees, as well as a guaranteed reliable pipeline for more of the same. That Bush brought Federalist Society members more frequently and more tightly into his judicial selection operations is not surprising: membership in its network was of proven value and certifiable reliability. By naming staunchly conservative, as well as relatively *young* candidates who promised long years of service on the bench, Bush solidified the ideological dominance of the federal judiciary begun by Reagan. The proof is in the numbers: by January 2009 and the close of the Reagan–Bush era of judicial appointment, 59 percent of all federal judges were GOP appointees and constituted solid majorities on ten of the thirteen courts of appeals.[6]

One question that occurs is whether Democratic presidents, post Reagan, have a similarly potent ideological network to draw on for their judicial selection staff and their judicial candidates. One could point to the American Constitution Society for Law and Policy, founded at Georgetown Law School in 2001 as a counterweight to the Federalist Society. ACS shares many institutional features with the latter: a nationwide network of law student and lawyers chapters, sponsorship of debates and conferences as a means to spread its progressive legal ideology, an annual convention featuring keynote speakers who are well-known liberal legal elites. (Justice Ginsburg was the featured speaker in 2012.) But ACS is young still, with its most prominent members—such as Obama's former Attorney General Eric Holder—having made their reputations before the organization existed. As such, it has yet to establish itself as the kind of legal personnel pipeline that Democratic presidents could tap into to "certify" their staffing and nominee choices. ACS does have a dedicated webpage to judicial nominations and their politics (Judicialnominations.org), but it operates more like a liberal watchdog or even a cheerleader and less like an intellectual society for the grooming and credentialing of liberal and progressive minded legal policy makers.

Like Carter before him, Democrat Barack Obama's emphasis in judicial staffing was on diversity (including, interestingly, experiential diversity), and less on a particular legal policy vision. While this agenda colored his judicial selections, it did not particularly affect his judicial selection machinery. Like Bush his immediate predecessor, Obama also empowered his White House Counsel's Office in judicial selection matters, particularly in conducting candidate interviews and orchestrating mock hearings sessions. As Elliot Slotnick and his coauthors summarized it in their 2015 study "Writing the Book of Judges": "the White House is dominant in the political facets of evaluation and advocacy [of nominees], particularly in working directly with the senators, while the work of the DOJ/OLP participants is more focused on professional evaluation of a candidate's qualifications" (Slotnick et al. 2015, 338). Under Obama, there was no formalized "Judicial Selection Committee" with regularized meetings; rather, key players from the Counsel's Office and OLP engaged in ongoing informal interactions.

Thus continuing the WHO-centric trend, Obama's first term political team on screening and staffing was headed by his chief of staff Rahm Emanuel and his longtime political aide and adviser David Axelrod. Also and somewhat unusually, Obama's vice president, Joe Biden, and Biden's chief of staff figured importantly in screening potential nominees; this was of course because of Biden's previous experience as Chair of the Senate Judiciary Committee. Not coincidentally, perhaps, one of Obama's two appointees to the Supreme Court, at the time his Solicitor General Elena Kagan, had served as Chairman Biden's special counsel and had helped usher Justice Ginsburg through the confirmation process. This episode, and the importance to the president of persons such as Axelrod, suggests the role that personal loyalty played in the politics of the Obama administration and in making up the Obama White House and judicial selection staff. Strong personal loyalty relations—including with pre-White House associates—can somewhat mitigate the influence of a Washington-based ideological network, like that of ACS, on presidential administration decisions. This seems to have been the case for Obama's judicial staffing decisions, as the president drew for his judicial selection staff on a traditional Democratic Party network of operatives: Clinton White House veterans, former campaign officials, progressively oriented university intellectuals.

Their personal and partisan commitment to Obama, however, did not extend to the concerted pursuit of an Obama policy agenda for the courts. There was simply no equivalent to the passionate commitment to the conservative legal cause that the Federalist Society facilitated in Republican staffers. As a result, one pattern that emerges from the Obama era was the eschewing of the bundling strategy for judicial nominations—even when plentiful, first term presidential political capital and a favorable Senate majority would have made the tactic a winning one. Journalistic accounts contend that it took the Obama administration several years to make judicial appointments a real priority; the liberal interest group Alliance for Justice called his first term "a missed opportunity" to fully staff the federal courts. One account charged that not until his White House Counsel Kathryn Ruemmler did Obama have a staffer fully committed to judicial staffing, and she served less than three years, only assuming her post in 2011. Criticisms have since softened, with the aforementioned Alliance remarking, by 2015, that expectations had been "exceeded" and that the president had done much better on than anyone expected, given the unprecedented obstruction that he had faced. Obama and his judicial selection staff certainly did make major accomplishments in appointing women and racial and ethnic minority judges to the federal courts, with approximately 60 percent of his appointees being "non-traditional," that is, not white males. And as a recent study by political scientist Robert Carp demonstrates, Obama's judges have a noticeably more liberal-voting record than do those appointed by fellow Democrat Bill Clinton[7] —who was, of course, hampered by an opposition-party-controlled Senate (not to mention impeachment proceedings) for much of his presidency. Still, Obama's eventual success in placing judicial candidates who furthered his presidential agenda largely depended on the work of his party's Senate

Majority Leader, and not on his White House judicial selection operations. Indeed, Sen. Harry Reid's 2013 filibuster reform for lower federal court nominees refocused an Obama administration that had let these nominations languish on a back burner, and allowed Obama's appointments to catch up to mounting judicial vacancies.[8] This ended with the Democrats' loss of the Senate in 2014, leaving Obama's final two years in office a study in Senate inaction on presidential nominations.

What relevant lessons can be learned from Bush and Obama's respective accomplishments, or lack thereof, with respect to shaping the personnel of the federal judiciary? The short answer is that the Reagan template is effective, but it depends on a level of energy and commitment that can be difficult to generate and sustain. That not all presidents come to their office with judicial appointments as a high priority is apparent. The Republican presidents of the 1980s through the 2000s were obviously highly motivated to develop the federal courts as an underutilized and unexploited policy arm, and their added fuel to this fire came from conservative legal movement activists—within and outside their administrations—who felt and felt intensely that existing legal policy and constitutional interpretation had been too heavily influenced by a liberal political agenda.

What burning desire Democrat Barack Obama felt with respect to the federal judiciary was encapsulated in the demographic diversity his appointees represented. This desire, and this accomplishment, should not be belittled: rather, it shows a clear presidential commitment to following through on a presidential agenda item, for the judiciary. It might also be fair to claim, as some journalistic accounts have, that Obama's diversity agenda was logistically incompatible with judicial selection streamlining efforts and assembly-lining tactics such as bundling of nominees. But Obama was neither part of nor the beneficiary of an ideological movement or network with respect to law and courts, which is why there was no candidate development well he could repeatedly go to. Much of his politico-legal agenda, as a Democrat, consisted in protecting and preserving an individual rights-based body of constitutional law. He and his White House and Justice

Department staff lacked the emergency-nature fervor of their GOP counterparts, on the matter of judicial staffing. Of course, as Republican-appointed judges have been retracting civil rights and voting rights protections while facilitating the political power of corporations and wealth in general, Democratic partisans may find more urgency in the project of shaping the composition of the federal courts. Making policy-oriented judicial appointments is an investment, but it also requires the same.

The "New Normal" of Presidential Administration of the Judicial Appointment Power

The rather unsurprising conclusion to this chapter of this presidential briefing book is that screening and staffing for judicial selection matter. And as is illustrated by the lessons extrapolated from the George W. Bush and Barack Obama records, such efforts are—or should be—the new normal for chief executives.

Adapting the twin, core components of candidate screening and executive staffing to a president's own individual circumstances is neither autonomic nor guaranteed of success. The Reagan template works best with a recirculating pipeline of candidates for both staff and judicial positions. It also reflects a mindset about the policy link between the presidency and the judiciary that has, to date, been better developed in Republican than Democratic Party circles. But even the most committed and ideological network-advantaged president must live in the contextual reality of same- versus opposite-party Senate. All presidents are now used to proactive preparation of potential nominee lists, in advance and in anticipation of vacancies opening; presidents should also fine-tune their proactive list making for Senate party control changing versus not changing. The political climate of the judicial appointment process is, as Chapter 1 on "History" concluded, contentious, polarizing, and frustrating. Of course, so is the political climate generally, in our decided non-bipartisan contemporary nation. Contemporary presidents, then, facing senates controlled by the opposition may be wisely advised *not* to divert their White House judicial selection resources to other topics in the presidential agenda (lest they be "money down the drain") but, instead, to reorient these resources and to reorient their own judicial staffing goals.

Obama's emphasis on the politically saleable diversity of his judicial candidates, instead of their ideology or policy orientation (of course, often the qualities nicely align), might be a good example of such White House reorientation—except that Obama pursued this appointment goal when he *enjoyed* the *asset* of same-party Senate control. Admittedly, his diversity candidates ran into sustained opposition from minority Republican senators, anyway. A challenge, surely, for a president's judicial selection staff, to identify a quality to seek in prospective nominees that is valuable to the president as well as defensively smart. Challenging, but not insurmountable, as the Obama nomination and 68–31 confirmation of Sonia Sotomayor indicates. Whether this first Latina justice would have confirmed by or even nominated under the condition of a GOP-controlled Senate is, of course, debatable, for only nine of the forty Republican senators voted to confirm her appointment. As one of the more common, "no" voting senators explained, "an excellent resume and an inspiring life story are not enough to qualify one for a lifetime of service on the Supreme Court . . . an individual who does not appreciate the common sense limitations on judicial power in our democratic system of government ultimately lacks a key qualification for a lifetime appointment to the bench." With this comment, Sen. John McCain was apparently forgetting that Sotomayor was already sitting on the federal bench, having been initially placed there by George H. W. Bush. But he was also attempting to deflect the undeniable force of the diversity qualification. Even so, one can presume that the "Justice Department in exile" during the Obama years was busily cultivating a supply of demographically diverse conservative lawyers with which to stock a future Republican president's prospective nominee list—especially should that president confront a Democratic Senate, whose majority members would have great difficulty opposing multicultural judicial candidates. Future Clarence Thomases, however, will likely not wear the

Federalist Society coat of arms so brazenly on their sleeves. That cat is out of the bag.

Still and all, the Republican domination of the federal courts and the concomitant conservative judicial decision making that has occurred over the last several decades—accomplished both under the noses and in the face of Democratic resistance—should convince Democratic as well as Republican presidents to invest in a sophisticated judicial selection operation when setting up their respective administrations. For more as to why this is so, we turn to the final chapter.

Notes

1. So quipped Attorney General Robert F. Kennedy, in speaking of senatorial courtesy practices and senatorial patronage actions with respect to the appointment of federal appellate and district court judges.
2. Joan Biskupic recounts this story in her recent book, *Breaking In: The Rise of Sonia Sotomayor and the Politics of Justice* (2014).
3. An election in which, some argued, the GOP-appointed justices of the Supreme Court joined together and played a key role, in the decisive ruling of *Bush v. Gore* (2000). The decision brought an end to controversial vote counting procedures for contested ballots in the Florida election returns, resulting in a Bush numerical victory and the state's electoral college votes, tipping the presidential election to Bush.
4. This episode is documented in Farganis and Wedeking, *Supreme Court Confirmation Hearings and the U.S. Senate: Reconsidering the Charade* (2014), at pp. 114–5.
5. Such as John Roberts' now well-known but somewhat misleading metaphor of the judge (and himself) as an "umpire."
6. George W. Bush did have his difficulties and suffer his defeats, as the Senate filibuster crisis of 2005 and several high-profile failed judicial candidacies illustrate. While the first was ultimately averted, the second can only be seen as an example of poor presidential judgment. See Chapter 2 "Candidates" for further discussion.
7. As noted by the news site Vox.com. (http://www.vox.com/2014/4/17/5617730/study-on-economics-obamas-judges-are-unusually-liberal)
8. For further discussion, see Chapter 3 "Context."

FIVE

Why

As previous chapters have detailed, it is certainly possible for a president to populate the courts with political and/or ideological adherents who can ensure that the president's legacy extends long beyond his or her term in office. This final chapter argues that it is also desirable if not mandatory for the modern, effective, and accountable president to do so.

A review of the historical development of the president's Article II appointment power shows that the capacity for both presidential discretion and leadership to operate has grown. That discretion is over options to pursue, and that leadership is about opportunities to be seized. By attending to the partisan dynamics of the institutional context of the federal appointment process, a president reduces the political uncertainty as to the confirmation prospects of his or her putative nominees. By carefully screening candidates for judicial nomination for the appropriate mix of qualifications, a president reduces informational uncertainty about their decision making as putative appointees. And a president further reduces uncertainty as to the confirmability, potential electoral consequences, and future decisional performance of his/her judicial appointments by assembling a diligent and savvy judicial selection staff in the White House and Justice Department, who can both identify candidates and provide support services for nominees during the period of senatorial scrutiny. Success is not the art of the possible; it lies in careful planning for the possible.

What also makes "packing" the courts possible and desirable is the empirical predictability and empirical validity of policy-oriented judicial behavior. Called the attitudinal model of judicial behavior and developed and tested by political scientists, this policy-oriented model of judging holds that judges "make decisions by considering the facts of the case in light of their ideological attitudes and values" (Segal and Spaeth 1993, 73). American judges implement, through interpretation and construction of law, their personal policy preferences. There is nothing nefarious in this, if we remember that federal judges are selected by a process necessarily inflected with politics and that "policy making involves choosing among alternative courses of action, where the choice binds the behavior of those subject to the policy maker's action" (p. 4). Legal decision making is policy making, about legal policies and legal rules. Judges fashion these, with their choices as to a legal policy's content or a legal rule's breadth informed by the alternatives that they themselves value or prioritize. As US Supreme Court Chief Justice Charles Evans Hughes famously declared, "we are under a Constitution, but the Constitution is what the judges say it is." Judicial scholar and political scientist Keith Wittington largely echoes this, observing that "judicial supremacy consists of the ability of the Supreme Court to erase the distinction between its own opinions interpreting the Constitution and the actual Constitution itself" (Whittington 2007, xi).

Presidential appreciation of the tenets of this attitudinal model of judicial decision making can pay dividends for him or her in the short and the long term. The next section reviews recent research asserting the increasing importance of ideology in nomination and confirmation of federal judges and assessing the accuracy of presidential assessment of judicial appointees' policy preferences. While the findings of social science studies are never completely dispositive, these provide further ammunition to the argument as to why "court packing" can and should be a presidential policy-making aspiration.

The final section and the briefing book conclude with the observation that the reality in the American political system and its method of judicial selection is that the Supreme Court follows the election returns. But the president has a role in managing that this happens, at the right time and in the right way, from the perspective of the president's own electoral mandate. If, in due course, the federal courts' personnel mirrors the political party that controls the national government—if elections truly have consequences—then presidents are obliged to use those resources at their disposal to exert the influence of their office to the best of their ability. The outcome is neither presidential dominance of government, nor judicial supremacy wielded by ideologues; it is, instead, the inevitable and appropriate result of the American idea of law as something shaped by changing coalitions of policy interests and contemporary conceptions of the public good.

Judges, Their Attitudes, and Their Decisions

Chapter 2 explored the mix of qualities that a president looks for in his or her judicial nominees; in that discussion, it was abundantly clear that political ideology and policy preferences, alongside professional and legal qualifications, inform presidential selection of candidates for the federal courts. It has ever been so, beginning with the presidency of George Washington, as Chapter 1 narrated. So there is nothing shocking about the proposition that judicial nomination—and confirmation—is done with an eye to the prospective judge's perceived ideology and expected liberal or conservative direction of voting once joining the federal bench.

The broad assertions of the attitudinal understanding of judicial decision making must be distinguished, however, from the actual scope of policy-oriented judging. It is one thing to posit, as a matter of theory, that federal judges vote their sincere policy preferences; it is another thing to say they always can and do. Two illustrative points are worth making here. First, the concept of measurable judicial ideology does not mean that all judges are ideologues, or even predominantly of an "ideological" political nature, as judges. Second, institutional and other kinds of role-orientation constraints affect judicial expression of personal attitudes about policy, legal, and otherwise. Presidents should attend to both of these points, lest they make ill-considered selections and have unrealistic expectations about them.

The concept of measurable judicial ideology, the methodological foundation of the attitudinal model of judging, simply means that judges can be arrayed along a left–right continuum by observing the patterns of judicial voting in cases. Judges' "display" of their sincerely held policy preferences, then, lies in the behavioral patterns they exhibit as a result of their aggregated votes. The content of judicial ideology is inferred from the presence of a behavioral pattern with respect to the direction of voting or the tendency of casting certain kinds of votes. The strength of ideology as a motivating force is further suggested by the consistency and recurring frequency of the behavioral pattern. For instance, how often and in what range of cases and fact situations does a judge support the government over the individual or a business corporation over the government? If supporting the governmental or corporate litigant is defined as "conservative" (i.e., yielding conservative policy outcomes), then the judicial tendency to do so equals conservative judicial voting behavior. A recurring and pervasive tendency to do so implies a strongly held and highly operative conservative policy orientation. Various innovations and sophistications in measuring judicial ideology have occurred in academic political science, such that a baseline ideological score can be estimated and then tested against other empirical evidence—like judicial voting data—to evaluate the predictive validity of attitudes for explaining judging.

Both baseline ideological scores and behavioral patterns reveal that most judges are neither wholly liberal nor conservative and that "moderate" is a possible judicial ideology. But this is not to say that attitudinal selection of judges is a hollow hope. It may be in a president's interest—a centrist president's interest, for instance—to seek judicial candidates who will *not* exhibit strongly leftward or rightward ideologically patterned voting across all issues coming before them. And if most judges are not absolute in their expressed ideology, then, well, ideology is not absolutely everything, in judging. Judges do not make legal policy solely by virtue of their votes in favor of petitioner or respondent, whomever those parties might be as litigants. Rather, judges' importance as legal policy makers—their value as presidential appointees—lies in the content of their decisions, in the legal rules described in their written opinions. While types of rhetoric and specific kinds of arguments may be associated with a particular ideological predilection, neither the force of rhetoric nor the power of argument is produced by ideologically patterned voting alone, however reliable that pattern. And neither rhetorical juristic force nor powerful judicial argument is subsumable under strength of a judge's ideology. Judicial ideology is separate and distinct from judicial persuasiveness or persuasive and influential legal policy making. While a president of course needs a like-minded majority to make an authoritative legal ruling in the first place, not all like-minded appointees are created equal in their capacity to use the written judicial opinion and judge-made legal doctrine to convince legal peers, audiences, and consumers of the correctness of their decisions. At times, then, a president must weigh measurable ideological "fit" against this larger, more impactful, but more woolly notion of "fitness."

Judicial ideology—its expression and its expected performance—is also deeply contingent upon an environment of extra-, inter-, and intra-court constraints. Neither the influence nor the aspect of judicial ideology is as black or white in judicial decisions as the attitudinal model of judging purports. Similarly, judges' ability to exhibit their potential for ideology-based decision making turns on their institutional position within the federal judicial hierarchy and the separation of powers structure. Lower federal court judges are simply more constrained by professional, hierarchical rule-following norms, like adhering to Supreme Court and circuit precedents on the application of statutes and the meaning of the Constitution. Their capacity to "be" ideologically motivated is limited by their institutional position and concern for their professional reputation—and, so, by any ambition they might have for higher judicial office. Conversely, Supreme Court justices are more free agents when it comes to drawing on their policy preferences in interpreting law: no court can overrule and thus discipline them. So too, the understanding of separation of powers is that the Court is supreme and plenary in its judicial branch authority over constitutional interpretation.[1]

For the highly salient and highly policy-charged controversies that constitutional cases are, Supreme Court justices operate in a relatively unconstrained environment, inter- and extra-court speaking. And while much is often made of the small group decision making dynamics on multi-member appellate courts, intra-court constraints—or the impediments raised by fellow judges who must be convinced into decisional and opinion coalitions—can be lubricated by ideological like-mindedness. Still, once solid ideological blocs can be fractured by new issues to be decided, and issue evolution can stir a justice to rethink a settled ideological stance and thus be more susceptible to colleagues' arguments and influence. Presidents cannot anticipate the specifics of any of this. Nevertheless, presidents must realize that intra-court judicial interactions can dampen the driving force of individual judicial ideologies—including individual ideologies that the president was confident in and counting on.

Any single-variable model of human behavior risks being reductionist, and the attitudinal model of judging is no different. When stated in the extreme, it presents the process of judicial decision making as overly simplistic, if not borderline inappropriate to the task of impartially resolving disputes and interpreting and applying legal rules. It is therefore important to remember that judging in America is a craft with its own professional canons, that judicial independence (of the federal courts, at least) is structurally provided by guaranteed life tenure in office, and that judges and courts—particularly the US Supreme Court—mind their own institutional legitimacy by engaging in strategic self-restraint. This can include following precedential decisions with which a judge does not personally agree so as to maintain stability in the law, ruling in accordance with precedent and against the political wishes of the president and/or political party that supported a judge's selection, and obeying collegial court dynamics and decisional norms of consensus over any political agenda. Presidents, even when they select a candidate on the basis of political ideology, (should) know this to be true. While cloning and nominating themselves is the dream, presidents are nominating their *jurist* selves, which is a slightly different matter.[2]

What presidents generally do *not* do—and have not done, consistently, for the last several decades—is select judicial nominees who are *incompatible* with the president's political ideology. Using a sophisticated methodology to estimate judicial and appointing presidential ideology (or "ideal points" in a left-to-right ideological space), a recent study holds that "Supreme Court justices carry their president's ideological commitments into their decisions, and that trend may be on the rise." This is especially true in an appointee's first few terms of service; by ten years out, there is a substantial decrease in the association or correlation between the president's and his or her justices' ideologies (Fifth Annual American Judicature Society Symposium 2008, 634–5). Political scientists call this "drift" and admit that despite the best presidential efforts, "the Alito and Roberts of today may not be the Alito and Roberts of tomorrow." Still, in a comparative sense, contemporary justices, even more than their predecessors, are entrenching their president's views into law, and long after he or she leaves office.

What this suggests is with sufficient information available, presidents can be reasonably accurate in assessing the policy preferences of (and their exhibition by) their judicial nominees. This is testimony to the worth of the extensive judicial selection apparatus documented and recommended in Chapter 4. In the words of one recent study of presidential "predictions" about their Supreme Court nominees, "the degree of congruence between the policy preferences of nominating presidents and the policies adopted by the justices they select" is "a function of the *quality* of information available to the president" (Szmer and Songer 2005, 153 [emphasis added]). Prior experience in the president's own administration, as well as prior law school teaching experience, provides the president with the highest quality, most accurate information with which he or she and his or her staff "may estimate the policy preferences of potential nominees" (p. 159). Even more than the record of decision making from appellate court, legislative, or other executive staff experience, administration advisers and publishing law school professors have revealed *with candor* their true views, legal and political, and can thus be counted on more reliably to continue to exhibit them on the bench. The quality of their argument, their ability to be persuasive, too, can be assessed—albeit subjectively—from the product they leave behind: memos, briefs, journal articles. It should come as no surprise to learn, then, that recent, successful appointing presidents—successful in the sense of enjoying that high degree of congruence in preferences between themselves and their appointees—have drawn heavily for their judges from the cohort of former and current advisers and ideologically sympathetic legal academics.

Somewhat ironically, it is also the case that what is possible, and desirable, to do quickly becomes the expected to do. No president can afford to dismiss or disregard what his or her predecessors have done, in the judicial appointment department. One's short-term political capital and one's long-term political reputation depends on replicating that success.

It is not only that there is an arms race quality to judicial appointments, in that once one's predecessor(s) has packed the courts, there is no incentive for the new president not to—or to place judicial staffing last on the list of political priorities, or to select proponents and practitioners of judicial modesty or some politically nonaligned version of judicial deference. One must respond in kind. There is also the pressure to perform in the office of chief executive and to use one's powers to the fullest capacity to express and promote one's own policy vision. Specific legal policy outcomes are of course desires specific to particular chief executives and their party regimes, and not all presidents find that changing the legal and/or constitutional status quo is high on the political agenda. A president might be content to let legal policy making and its constitutional precedents continue as is; his or her constituency might be less motivated by gains or claims in this area. But it would be a mistake for a president to neglect the courts and his or her political legacy there. Naming like-minded judges is the surest and most enduring policy vehicle a president can manage; and while it might seem at the time that there is no pressing need to secure a legal policy victory, carefully selected and well-placed federal judges *establish a policy bulwark* on a broad range of public policy issues from civil rights to economic regulation to executive authority. Offensive, defensive, or preemptive—the president who puts this bulwark into place will be the president noted for his or her forethought and remembered for his or her broad range of political ambition. To show little interest in or aptitude for such expansive political action is to risk becoming a premature irrelevancy.

It is hard to imagine, one Canadian jurist mused, a facet of American existence that has not been subjected to constitutional—and, thus, judicial—scrutiny. Judicial policy-making authority is pervasive—more pervasive, indeed, than presidential authority. And, as judicial scholars Harold Spaeth and Jeff Segal crisply note, since the *Bush v. Gore* decision awarding the presidency to George Bush, "everyone not totally disconnected from reality now recognizes that 'Judges make law'" (1993, 10). Better to be the one who had a hand in their appointment than the one solely on the receiving end of their wielding of judicial power.

Presidents, Their Judges, and Their Political Regimes

Of course, nothing is certain, lest of all judicial selection decisions. Mistakes happen—as Dwight Eisenhower famously remarked about his two appointees to the Supreme Court (clearly a case of poor-quality information being provided). Moreover, judicial drift from a president's and a party's issue constellation can happen sooner rather than later. The president who is an attentive student of the attitudinal model of judging can still be burned by an unforeseen policy question turned legal nightmare: presidents certainly cannot anticipate all of the future issues that will come before the federal courts, let alone how their appointees will (or even should) vote.

Having said this, it nevertheless remains the case that partisan political cycles in American electoral processes are generally reproduced in the staffing of the federal judiciary. Political regimes—defined as reigning political coalitions of ideology, interests, and commitments and the sets of government institutions and purposes they inherit—are expressed in electoral politics and in turn replicated in judicial appointees who share the regime political vision. Political regimes entrenched through judicial appointments can outlast or post-date that regime's electoral representation or existence. There is, in other words, lag time that can exist between the composition of the federal courts and rapid electoral change. But not all electorally driven policy innovation will necessarily provoke judicially relevant problems, for "the implications of electoral change for judicial action depend heavily on the particular substance of dominant institutional and policy commitments" (Whittington 2007, 43). Some institutional and policy commitments are so dominant as to transcend political regimes, to cross partisan electoral shifts; some are also deeply imbedded in a constitutional or constitutional law regime. (Many, of course, are not.) Political incentives lead presidents to choose either to challenge or to defer to the court's constitutional leadership. "Reconstructive" presidents—those who truly seek to dismantle inherited constitutional and ideological norms and build a new political regime—are those who defy the judicial branch and assert their own presidential authority to construct a new constitutional order. They do not pack the courts so much as attempt to circumvent them. But such presidents are few and far between in political time. The more commonplace electoral cycle and more normal presidential stance is to use the courts and presidential appointments to them as a legal policy-making auxiliary, and even a pressure safety valve—by devolving to courts and to their constitutional/legal judgment those policy questions too politically contentious or potentially costly to control and decide from the law-making branches.[3]

A president's mandate is electoral, it should be expressed in the presidential agenda, and to a large extent service of this mandate is not optional. The president who wants to be reelected, the president who wants to secure election for his or her party successor, and the president who wants to establish and extend the longevity of his or her political regime understands this. That president also understands that his or her mandate applies to the federal judiciary and its staffing as well, and is likewise a mandate fidelity to which is not optional. Presidential accountability to the popular mandate, to his or her political regime, thus can unite with the operative reality that the courts follow the election returns by virtue of the political nature of their process of appointment.

When the courts are perceived as too highly politicized, however, judicial authority—as well as presidential opportunity to mold the content and the contours of that authority—is weakened. A newspaper editorial, contemporaneous with the writing of this presidential briefing book, had this to say about the current Supreme Court:

> [It] has become a more partisan institution in recent decades, more closely resembling the other branches of government than it once did . . . the current court is the first one in American history in which close, major cases regularly feature all of the Democratic appointees and all of the Republican ones on opposite sides . . . An increasingly partisan, polarized country would have a Supreme Court moving in a similar direction." (Leonhardt 2015)

A president's responsibility in such an increasingly partisan, polarized environment is to make sure that the interests of his or her electoral coalition are reflected in the *selection* of federal judges. But a president must decide, as a matter of statesmanship, how closely and minutely those partisan interests should be reflected in the *judges* selected.

Still and all, the most successful presidents, the presidents to emulate, are those who earn the distinction of a court era named after them. These are the presidents who claim the authority to act on their own independent understandings of the Constitution and subsequently install members of the federal judiciary who share and will perpetuate the substance of that understanding. Scholars speak of the Roosevelt Court or the Reagan judiciary, because these presidents utilized their executive appointive powers to extend the reach and the policy significance of their respective political regimes. Numbers of appointees were part of that reach and significance, but not the only element. Legal and ideological quality of appointees, attention to their vetting and selection, aggressive embrace of the judicial branch as a policy arm of the president's political regime—these attributes and actions, in addition to the sheer numbers of judges placed, were critical to the presidential record of success. Franklin Roosevelt and Ronald Reagan—however else we remember them and in whatever ways they are otherwise similar or different—they appreciated and approached court packing as possible, desirable, and necessary for an efficacious presidency, short and long term. While not itself sufficient to be considered an effective president, such presidential action leaves a legacy of nomenclature for a reason. Beyond the decorative honor of depiction on the nation's currency, picking judges is the closest most presidents can come to political immortality. Neither pictorial nor policy resemblance is indelible, of course,[4] but the latter—united with the judicial authority to carry that policy out—pays greater dividends of more enduring value for a president's remembered legacy, in the end.

Notes

1. The Court's own (unchallenged) assertions to this effect can be found in decisions from *Marbury v. Madison* (1803) to *Cooper v. Aaron* (1958) to *City of Borne v. Flores* (1997).
2. The example of William Howard Taft is instructive—the only person to serve both as President of the United States and then (Chief) Justice on the Supreme Court. As a reluctant and single-term president, Taft nonetheless had the opportunity to nominate an all-time record six justices to the high bench, including the chief justice. He strategically selected sitting associate Edward White, hoping that actuarial fortunes would be in Taft's favor and that he would outlive his choice and thus be available to replace him. His greatest life wish finally came true in 1921 when he was appointed by Republican president Warren G. Harding.

   Taft's political self was loyally Republican and somewhat conservative, particularly on many of the labor and social issues of the day. As a jurist, however, he presented a more dynamic conservatism, endorsing national commercial regulations as long as they did not compromise the sanctity and inviolability of his beloved institution's judicial decisions. "I love judges, and I love courts," Taft was known to have said, making him somewhat of an unusual chief executive in more than one regard.

3. Whittington calls this delegating to the federal courts the task of "regime elaboration and enforcement" and also notes how courts can be "called upon to reconcile competing strands of the inherited [political] regime." See p. 117 and p. 159, respectively.
4. At this writing, it would appear that President George W. Bush's Supreme Court justices may well outlast President Andrew Jackson's visage on the twenty-dollar bill.

BIBLIOGRAPHY

A list of recommended and cited sources.

Abraham, Henry. 1992. *Justices and Presidents*, 3rd ed. New York: Oxford University Press.

Abraham, Henry. 2008. *Justices, Presidents and Senators*, 5th ed. Lanham, MD: Rowman and Littlefield.

Avery, Michael, and Danielle McLaughlin. 2013. *The Federalist Society: How Conservatives Took the Law Back from Liberals.* Nashville, TN: Vanderbilt University Press.

Barrow, Deborah, and Thomas J. Walker. 1988. *A Court Divided: The Fifth Circuit Court of Appeals and the Politics of Judicial Reform.* New Haven, CT: Yale University Press.

Bell, Laura Cohen. 2002. *Warring Factions.* Columbus, OH: Ohio State University Press.

Binder, Sarah A., and Forrest Maltzman. 2009. *Advice and Dissent.* Washington, DC: The Brookings Institution.

Biskupic, Joan. 2014. *Breaking In: The Rise of Sonia Sotomayor and the Politics of Justice.* New York: Sarah Crichton Books, Farrar, Staus and Giroux.

Collins, Paul, and Lori Ringhand. 2013. *Supreme Court Confirmation Hearings and Constitutional Change.* New York: Cambridge University Press.

Comiskey, Michael. 2004. *Seeking Justices.* Lawrence, KS: University Press of Kansas.

Eisgruber, Christopher. 2007. *The Next Justice.* Princeton, NJ: Princeton University Press.

Epstein, Lee, William M. Landes, and Richard A. Posner. 2013. *The Behavior of Federal Judges.* Cambridge, MA: Harvard University Press.

Epstein, Lee, and Jeffrey Segal. 2005. *Advice and Consent.* New York: Oxford University Press.

Farganis, Dion, and Justin Wedeking. 2014. *Supreme Court Confirmation Hearings in the U.S. Senate: Reconsidering the Charade.* Ann Arbor, MI: University of Michigan Press.

Feldman, Stephen M. 2013. *Neoconservative Politics and the Supreme Court.* New York: New York University Press.

Fifth Annual American Judicature Society Symposium. Spring 2008. "The Intersection of Personal Convictions and Federal Judicial Selection." *Drake Law Review* 56 (3): 587–828.

Gibson, James, and Gregory Caldeira. 2009. *Citizens, Courts, and Confirmations.* Princeton, NJ: Princeton University Press.

Gillman, Howard. 1999. "The Court as an Idea, Not a Building (or a Game)." In *Supreme Court Decision-Making*, edited by C. Clayton and H. Gillman. Chicago, IL: University of Chicago Press.

Gillman, Howard, and Cornell Clayton, eds. 1999. *The Supreme Court in American Politics.* Lawrence, KS: University Press of Kansas.

Goldman, Sheldon. 1997. *Picking Federal Judges.* New Haven, CT: Yale University Press.

Hall, Kermit L. 1992. *The Oxford Companion to the Supreme Court of the United States.* New York: Oxford University Press.

Hettinger, Virginia, Stefanie Lindquist, and Wendy Martinek. 2006. *Judging on a Collegial Court.* Charlottesville, VA: University of Virginia Press.

Kahn, Michael, and Harry Pohlman. 2005. *May It Amuse the Court: Editorial Cartoons of the Supreme Court and the Constitution.* Athens, GA: Hill Street Press.

Klein, David E. 2002. *Making Law in the United States Courts of Appeals.* New York: Cambridge University Press.

Leonhardt, David. March 3, 2015. "A Polarized Court, Weighing a Reversal of the Safety Net." *The New York Times.*

Maltese, John A. 1995. *The Selling of Supreme Court Nominees.* Baltimore, MD: The Johns Hopkins University Press.

Massaro, John. 1990. *Supremely Political.* Albany, NY: State University of New York Press.

Mason, Alpheus Thomas. 1968. *The Supreme Court from Taft to Warren.* Baton Rouge, LA: Louisiana State University Press.

Maveety, Nancy. 2009. "Low Risk and Big Ambition: The Politics of George W. Bush's Judicial Appointments." In *Ambition and Division: The Presidency of George W. Bush*, edited by S. Schier. Pittsburgh, PA: University of Pittsburgh Press.

Maveety, Nancy. 2011. "A Transformative Politics of Judicial Selection? President Obama and the Federal Judiciary." In *Transforming America: Barack Obama in the White House*, edited by S. Schier. Lanham, MD: Rowman and Littlefield.

McMahon, Kevin. 2011. *Nixon's Court.* Chicago, IL: University of Chicago Press.

Nemacheck, Christine. 2008. *Strategic Selection: Presidential Nomination of Supreme Court Justices from Herbert Hoover through George W. Bush.* Charlottesville, VA: University of Virginia Press.

Pertschuk, Michael, and Wendy Schaetzel. 1989. *People Rising: The Campaign Against the Bork Nomination.* New York: Thunder's Mouth Press.

Peters, Jeremy. September 13, 2014. "Building Legacy, Obama Reshapes Appellate Bench." *The New York Times.*

Scherer, Nancy, and Banks Miller. June 2009. "The Federalist Society's Influence on the Federal Judiciary." *Political Research Quarterly* 62: 366–92.

Scherer, Nancy, Brandon Bartels, and Amy Steigerwalt. 2008. "Sounding the Fire Alarm: The Role of Interest Groups in the Lower Court Confirmation Process." *Journal of Politics* 70: 1026–39.

Schlesinger, Arthur. 1973. *The Imperial Presidency.* New York: Houghton Mifflin.

Schwartz, Herman. 1993. *A History of the Supreme Court.* New York: Oxford University Press.

Schwartz, Herman. January 13, 2014. "Filling Judicial Vacancies to Protect the Progressive Legacy." *Reuters.*

Segal, Jeffrey, and Harold Spaeth. 1993. *The Supreme Court and the Attitudinal Model.* New York: Cambridge University Press.

Segal, Jeffrey, and Harold Spaeth. 2002. *The Supreme Court and the Attitudinal Model Revisited.* New York: Cambridge University Press.

Shipan, Charles, and Megan Shannon. 2003. "Delaying Justice(s): A Durational Analysis of Supreme Court Confirmation." *American Journal of Political Science* 47: 654–68.

Shomade, Salmon, Roger Hartley, and Lisa Holmes. January 2014. "Lower Federal Court Judicial Confirmation Fights." *Political Science and Politics* 47: 149–64.

Silverstein, Mark. 2007. *Judicious Choices.* New York: W. & W. Norton.

Skowronek, Stephen. 2008. *Presidential Leadership in Political Time.* Lawrence, KS: University Press of Kansas.

Slotnick, Elliot, Sheldon Goldman and Sara Schiavoni. Fall 2015. "Writing the Book of Judges: Obama's Judicial Appointments Record after Six Years." *Journal of Law and Courts* 3: 331–67.

Southworth, Ann. 2008. *Lawyers of the Right.* Chicago, IL: University of Chicago Press.

Steigerwalt, Amy. 2010. *Battle over the Bench.* Charlottesville, VA: University of Virginia Press.

Szmer, John, and Donald Songer. March 2005. "The Effects of Information on the Accuracy of Presidential Assessments of Supreme Court Nominee Preferences." *Political Research Quarterly* 58: 151–60.

Teles, Steven. 2008. *The Rise of the Conservative Legal Movement.* Princeton, NJ: Princeton University Press.

Tomlins, Christopher, ed. 2005. *The United States Supreme Court.* New York: Houghton Mifflin.

Toobin, Jeffrey. October 27, 2014. "The Obama Brief." *The New Yorker.*

Whittington, Keith. 2007. *Political Foundations of Judicial Supremacy: The Presidency, the Supreme Court, and Constitutional Leadership in U.S. History.* Princeton, NJ: Princeton University Press.

Wittes, Benjamin. 2006. *Confirmation Wars.* Lanham, MD: Rowman and Littlefield.

Yalof, David. 1999. *Pursuit of Justices.* Chicago, IL: University of Chicago Press.